Voice and Style

Marc Connors of The Nylons

Angela F.M. Pancella

INFI∞ITY
PUBLISHING

Copyright © 2001 by Angela F.M. Pancella

ISBN 978-0-7414-0702-3

Published by:

INFINITY PUBLISHING
1094 New DeHaven Street, Suite 100
West Conshohocken, PA 19428-2713
Toll-free (877) BUY BOOK
Local Phone (610) 941-9999
Fax (610) 941-9959
Info@buybooksontheweb.com
www.buybooksontheweb.com

Printed in the United States of America

Published May, 2001

Acknowledgments

The person who is perhaps most directly responsible for this book is my mother. She didn't let me go on a road trip to see The Nylons for what turned out to be one of Marc's last performances. Because of this, I never saw Marc in concert and had to learn about him by asking all these questions of people who knew him. Thus, a book. Out of profound disappointment, a greater reward. Thanks, Mom.

And Ian Wallace—Nion—made the extraordinary decision to share Marc's journal and scrapbook and pictures and memorabilia with an 18-year-old writer who wanted to tell his story. This book is dedicated to him.

The following people assisted with this book directly or indirectly, and my profound thanks go out to all of them: Stephanie Bahr, Micah Barnes, Julie Brown, Paul Cooper, Kerry Dahlen, Jim Dreste, Jim Frewen, Jason Gillespie, Denise Hargrove, Ali Hegel, Jan Julien, Caroline Leslie, Jo Leslie, Carrie Lewis, Al Mair, Linda Mancini, Avis Meyer, Claude Morrison, Sue Morrison, Steve Multer, Lisa Niewoehner, Paolo Pace, Helen Pancella, Phyllis Pancella, Michael Paruch, Mary Reihing, Geoff Roberts, Reiko Saito, Chris Thomas, Bill Vincent, Karen Webb, and anyone I may have inadvertently forgotten.

Thanks also to the St. Louis Public Library for the use of their computers, and the Writers Under the Arch for their assistance and encouragement.

Table of Contents

Table of Content

Introduction

I was in the parking lot of a shopping mall with my sister Helen. I was 13. Out of the blue she started singing something about jungles and lions, a lullaby with a strange high chorus. "What song is that? Who sings it?"

"It's 'The Lion Sleeps Tonight,'" she told me. "I don't know who sings it."

At the end of the week, by strange coincidence, I heard that a Canadian a cappella group called The Nylons would present this song on "The Jim Henson Hour." So I watched. And now it's 12 years later, and I've written a book.

It's all because of the man singing the song that night, Marc Connors, who possessed a voice and a performance style that I think are still unparalleled.

Some of you who read this are already nodding your heads in agreement: Yes, Marc had something extraordinary. Others of you are saying "Who?" or "The Nylons—they had a hit, didn't they? That 'na na, hey hey, goodbye' song?"

If you knew Marc's work or saw him in concert, I hope this book gives you greater insight into his character. If you didn't know Marc or were just vaguely aware of him, I recommend you pick up a copy of any Nylons album he sang on (The Nylons, One Size Fits All, Seamless, Happy Together, Rockapella, or Four on the Floor). Listen to it as I introduce you to one of the finest talents I have ever come across.

I have worked on this book for about seven years. I was 18 when I officially set about writing it, three years after Marc's death. It is the first project of this scope I have ever undertaken. The complexity of the subject, as well as my inexperience, could have meant the project was doomed to fail. I consider it a kind of miracle that I have found so many people willing to share their memories of Marc in the profound, articulate fashion you will find here. I was not

i

able to talk with everyone I wished to talk to, nor was I able to fit all of the interviews I did conduct into the "narrative" that emerged. I hope someone may be inspired to tell Marc's story more fully; in the meantime, this book represents all I have learned.

A quick explanation of the structure: Originally I intended this to be a biography, where I would narrate the story of Marc's life using quotes from articles and interviews as needed. But after many conversations with Marc's friends, fans, and bandmates, I realized the people who knew Marc should tell his story themselves. So each interview is its own chapter. I have put in the questions I asked or other background information only when necessary for the sake of clarity. I have also included a chronology at the beginning, to help the reader put everything that is said into context.

The interviews are arranged roughly in the order of the portion of Marc's story they address. Obviously, there will be some repetition as different people recall the same events, although each recalls or emphasizes different aspects. This is fitting for the story of an a cappella singer. Marc's life becomes the song sung by a chorus of voices. Everyone's affection for him creates blend in the voices, and what could have been cacophony is instead harmony.

Towards the end Marc speaks directly, through some entries from a journal he kept. The last word comes from Ian Wallace. You will see why.

The Internet will be an additional resource in sharing Marc's story. I have posted pictures and more information that did not fit the scope of this book at www. voiceandstyle.com.

I have done my best to present everything here as accurately as possible. If you spot any errors, please write me care of the publisher or at apancella@hotmail.com, and I will make corrections to future editions.

One last note—When this book talks about The Nylons, it is chiefly in reference to Marc's time with the group, from its beginning until his death in 1991. Thus, I mostly use past tense when referring to The Nylons. This is only because I am using the group name as a shorthand way of saying "The Nylons as they existed from 1979 to 1991" and should not be taken to mean The Nylons are no more. In fact, at the time of this writing the group is still recording and touring, their career now a span of longer than 20 years—which is a remarkable accomplishment in the popular music world and, in itself, a tribute to Marc's vision.

Chronology

April 15, 1949: Marc Thomas Connors born to Captain Thomas Edward Connors and Yolande Chabot Connors in Ottawa, Ontario. He is the only son; his sisters are Marcia, Denise, and Collette.

The family lives in different cities in Marc's youth, settling for a time in Halifax, Nova Scotia, as the Navy moved Marc's father around. They return to Ottawa when Marc is 12.

"I always wanted to do something artistic. My grandmother was a vaudevillian in Quebec, billed as La Petite Augustine, and she gave me a love of entertaining."—Marc quoted in an article from a Halifax newspaper written by Nancy MacDonald, 7/29/83

"I was just attracted to fantasy. As a child I used to watch entertainment and absorb the characters and become...like, my mother used to ask me after watching movies, 'Well, who are you now?' I'd walk out and not even realize I'd be playing the character. I was just very attracted as an audience member to fiction on the stage, to drama. And singing and dancing just make it more so, more expressive."—Marc, quoted in "Connors Is a Four-in-One Bargain" by Phil Shaw, Ottawa Revue, May 1980

1963-1967: By this time Marc is attending St. Patrick's College High School, where his best friend is Chris Thomas.

April 1966: Marc wins a trophy, $100, a scroll of merit and a write-up in the local papers in a public speaking contest in Toronto. The topic of his speech: "World Federalism."

"My topic? Oh...'How to die of galloping consumption and love it.'"—Marc, years later captioning a photo from 1966 in his scrapbook.

1967: Marc is active in plays at Immaculata High School, the local girl's school. This year he wins a prize at the Centennial Drama Festival for Ottawa secondary schools: best supporting actor for his role as Christopher Wren in "The Mousetrap."

"We presented this play in October. It was lots of fun but the audience liked 'Gypsy' ['Gypsy Rover,' his first play at Immaculata] better...Then we got the exciting news—we were selected for the festival! We heard this in April. The performance was May 12...

The play was the most nervous two hours of my life. Then [actress Jennifer Phipps] came up on stage, we sat on stage too and she adjudicated. One by one she dealt with the people and then she turned to me and said 'I think there's only one left.' The audience gave me a standing ovation! Then she said things like...'this man can act. I'd like to see him in a dramatic role. He could hold a play...' Then we sat downstairs...and waited for the prizes. Best supporting actor: Marc Connors. People erupted around me. Another standing ovation! I just said 'Thank you, ladies and gentlemen, for honoring me so...so well.'"—Marc, from his scrapbook.

Travels to Miami for a Knights of Pythias-sponsored public speaking contest; wins a college scholarship.

1968: Forms his own drama troupe, the Skeleton Theatre, with Paul Kelman at Le Monde coffeehouse. He cites Jerzy Grotowski, Peter Brook, and the Tulane Drama Review as his inspirations, and envisions for a production of "Baal" that the entire theater-going experience—from the moment the tickets are taken—will become part of the performance.

"What we want mostly is imagination...Acting is a continual imaginative process."—Marc, quoted in a newspaper story about the Skeleton Theater.

Attends Glendon College at York University, intending to major in English.

1969: transfers to University of Alberta in Edmonton to study theatre arts. He will graduate from here in 1972 with a BFA in Drama. Here he will meet Cheryl Cashman. He will work with her in many experimental pieces she writes or directs, including "Yesterday the Children Were Dancing," "Say Goodbye to Brady," "Where is the Voice Coming From?" and "The Tempest," which is staged in the chancel of Holy Trinity Church in Toronto.

1971 and 1972: works at a summer theatre program in Fort Peck, Montana. He is King Arthur in "Camelot" and Cervantes/Don Quixote in "Man of La Mancha," among other things.

1972-1978: He takes on a variety of theatrical projects that lead him to cities across Canada. He is Leonidik in "The Promise" at Montreal's Centaur Theatre, Jesus in "Godspell" in a touring production. In 1974-5 he works in Stratford with the Young Stratford Company; in 1976 he and Martin Short are two stars in a revue called "Harry's Back in Town" where Peter Mann, later The Nylons' main arranger, is the musical director. In 1977 he performs in the Charlottetown Festival on Prince Edward Island in "Legend of the Dumbells" (the story of a crossdressing comedy troupe who entertained Canadian troops in World War I) and "By George!" as well as "Anne of Green Gables."

Marc meets Ian Wallace in 1974 when they were both part of Robin Phillips' "Young Company" at Stratford. The two of them become lovers. Afterward Marc spends four months backpacking in Europe, where he sees and is greatly inspired by Le Theatre de Soleil; he returns to join Ian in Ottawa and works with Linda Rabin in the dance program at Richard Pochinko's Theatre Resource Center.

Marc, Ian and Richard remain close throughout their lives and will each take a turn in charge of the Theatre Resource Centre.

Marc receives a Canada Council grant to study singing at the Royal Conservatory of Music in Toronto. He also indulges his passion for dance by choreographing and co-starring in a nightclub act called "Marcus and Meira."

"Emerging from this [TRC experience] he was so fired up...that Connors decided the just wanted to do something crazy. Teamed with a friend, a dancer in Les Grands Ballets, he developed a strip show that involved a variety of tableaux and a lot of good taste. Booked into a club in Gatineau (the duet discovered late in preparations that the club required full nudity, but they went ahead) the show was a great success. People said it was real theatre, real fantasy."
("Connors is a Four-in-One Bargain")

1977-1978: Marc meets Paul Cooper and Claude Morrison (he had already been friends with Denis Simpson) and the four of them begin singing together. At this time, as Marc is somewhat disenchanted with theatre life, he and Ian are working as cooks at the Queen Mother Café on Queen Street in Toronto.

"I was searching. I was looking for something. I'd tried just about everything that there was to do in Canadian theatre, and I wasn't really happy with any of it. One of the problems of being educated with a bachelor of fine arts degree is that they acquaint you with some of the more lofty names and ideals of theatre, and these people all seem so artistic and dedicated. Then when you get out into the working world, you encounter a lot of situations where someone's uncle owns the TV station, so he's got the lead role. You encounter little petty dictators. Et cetera. Et cetera. You have to face the fact that probably a lot of your dreams of great achievement in theatre will take a lot longer to realize than you thought. I went through a period of disillusionment, especially after appearing at Stratford. It was always held up that Stratford was summum bonum, the place that had the greatest standards. I don't know. It wasn't for me, anyway."—Marc, quoted in the Chicago Tribune, April 12, 1985

February 20, 1979: Calling themselves "The Nylons" in tongue-in-cheek tribute to "fabric" groups like The Chiffons and The Orlons, Marc, Paul, Claude and Denis sing four songs at a contest in an ice-cream restaurant called Scoops. They are a big hit.

"But nobody had taken the best synthetic of all!"—Marc explaining how the name was chosen in a USA Today feature in 1987

May 16, 1979: The Nylons, with Ralph Cole as bass instead of Denis Simpson, perform at a new cabaret begun by Taras Shipowick called Van Sloten's Cabaret (on Dundas Street West, just across from the Art Gallery of Ontario). It is so new it has yet to get a liquor license. (The torch from Ralph to Denis, by the way, was passed at a club called Pear's. There were five Nylons on stage that night.) Audience and media response to the new act is unprecedented and almost unbelievable. The act is held over for six weeks.

By October they are featured on CBC Radio, CHUM FM, CKFM, CKEY, Q-107, CBL, CBC TV, CFTO TV, and CITY TV.

"The Nylons, an unaccompanied male quartet, come on stage in punk jackets and give a strong impression they're going to blast the world. But instead they deliver standards of the '40s, '50s, '60s and some '70s hits faithfully and some such as Bruce Springsteen's 'Fire' in a new arrangement that goes over to wild applause...And, despite some lapses in pitch, they're terrific and should do well in clubs."

("New Acts," Variety, July 4, 1979)

"They've melded together punk visuals (stark, dark contrasts denuded of color) [and] sexual playfulness (they don't hide a comfortable homosexual sensibility)...The music's the thing. The packaging and lifestyle are offered but not thrust on the audience. 'We don't lay down a trip,' explains Connors. 'The number is that there's no numbers. We just want everyone to have a good time...It's not political and I don't feel political. But the change for me is that we're being vulnerable. And I was scared at first. On-stage before I always played a role."

(Bruce Kirkland in the Toronto Star, June 21, 1979)

March 1981: Ralph Cole leaves the group and Arnold Robinson, who had performed with members of the Platters and had been in music management, becomes the new bass singer. The Nylons' lineup will be Marc Connors, Paul

Cooper, Claude Morrison and Arnold Robinson from this point until 1990.

"The attraction was the potential I saw in this odd form...I guess once a performer always a performer...In this type of group we are creating everything. We are the total energy...if we're not doing something, it's dead air."—Arnold, looking back at his start with The Nylons in an article by Kevin Prokosh.

1982: Their first album, simply called The Nylons, is released on the Canadian independent label Attic Records. It hits gold record status (50,000 copies sold) in a matter of weeks. As they had worked on the album prior to having a record label, The Nylons are able to release their second album, One Size Fits All, this year as well. (I have seen a single which predates The Nylons and includes "Some People [Song for Sheena]" and a song which never made it onto an album, "Mirage." It appeared to be released by The Nylons on their own, so perhaps it predates their record contract.) The Nylons features as many original songs as covers like "The Lion Sleeps Tonight" and "Up on the Roof," an early testament to their desire to be taken seriously as songwriters as well as song interpreters. One Size Fits All makes use of a drum machine throughout, showing their interest in rhythm as an essential component to their music. (The first album included percussion as well, mostly performed live by Arnold Robinson).

"We want to be on the cutting edge of things. If we take some of our repertoire from the '50s and '60s, it's because that music was based on vocals."—Marc, quoted in "Seamless Songs from the Street," a Nylons feature in Maclean's, March 9, 1982

1984: <u>Seamless</u> is released.

There are reports in the press around this time that The Nylons had run into financial trouble, which is downplayed by their manager, Wayne Thompson (also the manager of the Canadian Brass). The band did go into receivership for a short while as they looked for new investors. Paul Cooper had been mentioning plans for the group to make a musical version of the b-movie "Mars Needs Women," camped up in the style of "Rocky Horror Picture Show." These plans were abandoned, but one of the songs he wrote for the project becomes a highlight of <u>Seamless</u>: "The Stars are Ours."

"Debts were up to $450,000 owed to a variety of sources, from investors to American Express. Thompson, who had managed The Nylons since 1981, put Nylons Inc. into receivership. [Thompson says,] 'Nobody really understands what it costs to break an act worldwide with only a Canadian base. Even at home we lose money. In 1982 we did a Canadian tour that lost $140,000. This was not just us and a few microphones. We had our own semi and a crew of 14. Were we smart? I don't know. But we did learn. Our staging for The Roxy was great and fit into 2 suitcases.'"—from "Canadian Musicians and Their Money," a feature by Jonathan Gross in <u>Canadian Musician</u>.

By this time The Nylons has a distribution deal in the US with Windham Hill Records, who are mostly known for "New Age" style instrumentalists and mood musicians like George Winston, Night Noise, Shadowfax, etc. Windham Hill releases <u>One Size Fits All</u> and <u>Seamless</u> on their Open Air label, the former in 1983 and the latter in 1984. The US versions are different from the Canadian versions. "Bumble Boogie" was cut from <u>One Size Fits All</u> for its Stateside release, "Samba Samba" cut from <u>Seamless</u>. In addition, the track order for <u>Seamless</u> is completely rearranged, "Perpetual Emotion" and "Combat Zone" shortened, "Up on the Roof" added (as Windham Hill isn't distributing the first album) and "The Lion Sleeps Tonight" re-recorded.

1986: The Nylons plan to be the first Canadian act to perform in China, plans that apparently do not reach fruition, though they do perform in Japan, Australia, and Europe. They also win an award at the Tokyo Music Festival for their version of "Up the Ladder to the Roof." The prize money is one million yen, which in 1986 is worth about $7,800 Canadian dollars.

Marc and Ian are diagnosed HIV positive.

1987: The Nylons release Happy Together. The album yields a hit single in the Steam song "Kiss Him Goodbye," which reaches number 12 on the Billboard charts.

"While...Marc Connors said the group initially recoiled at the suggestion [to record 'Kiss Him Goodbye'], it discovered the song had a 'singable' verse. 'The other half of it is, yes, it's a popular tune. And (pausing) damn it, we don't always want to be shunted aside as "Oh, yeah, it's a cappella"', exclaimed Connors, his voice rising. 'We want to be up there (on the charts),' he said. 'We've been frustrated and we've been doing it a long time. And now it's time!...There's a realistic understanding that cover tunes are the ones that are picked up (on radio) by us. And there isn't a lot of time or respect placed on our original material even though I think it's very good. But make no mistake. We want to be commercial. When we have guaranteed sales of 500,000 to a million, then we can do something because we want to do it. Until that time, we just want to recoup our costs. But nobody wants to be a hack. We want to inject our personality and artistry into the music all the while we're trying to make it popular.'"

("The Nylons Break Out With Cover Tune," a 1987 article by Tim O'Connor picked up by the wire services)

1989: The Nylons release <u>Rockapella</u>. The long list of producers who are needed to bring this album to fruition reflects the conflict occurring in the band. Paul Cooper leaves The Nylons in November.

"Their latest album...will include...a new arrangement of 'Rise Up,' a hit three years ago for the popular Toronto band The Parachute Club. That song, says Connors, represents an interesting crossover for The Nylons...'For the rest of the world it's a new song, but for Canada it's a cover of an old classic.'"
["New Markets for Nylons," David Barber, 11/26/88]

1990: After extensive auditions, Micah Barnes joins the Nylons in February. By the end of the year Marc, Claude, Arnold and Micah are preparing a live album while Marc's health is beginning to decline dramatically.

Richard Pochinko dies of an AIDS-related illness.

Marc produces "A Starry Night," a tribute to Pochinko and a fundraiser for the Theatre Resource Center. The Nylons perform an early version of a new song by Connors, "Amazon," which deals directly with the destruction of the rain forest. Ian Wallace, as his clown character Nion, also performs.

1991: In the first part of February The Nylons perform their last concerts with Marc in Boise, Idaho. The group takes a vacation, and Marc and Ian go to Arizona to a healing spa. They return to Toronto in late March.

On March 25, Marc dies of viral pneumonia at the Bassett/Falk Oncology Centre in Toronto. AIDS is not mentioned in the first reports of his death, but Claude later confirms the media's suspicions in an interview.

"'I know Marc is still communicating with us,' says Nylon Claude Morrison...'Since he died I've been having dreams where he's speaking to me, guiding me to keep going, instructing me to what my next steps should be. Let me assure you that I'm rational, I'm sane, and I'm not religious. I sound so vacuously new-age, but I can hear his voice as though he is actually speaking to me. I've jolted awake in the middle of the night and I see him standing by my bed. It sounds crazy, but it's real. I can't explain it.'...Morrison is quick to link the disease that took Connors' life with the present state of the environment. 'The Earth has AIDS. The St. Lawrence River has cancer. The Pacific coastline has pneumonia. The Brazilian Amazon is packed with lesions. I think it's an apt analogy. AIDS and the environment are one and the same cause, in a sense.'"—from a Vancouver newspaper article by Sheila Morrison in May of 1991

The live album <u>Four on the Floor</u> is released with a dedication to Marc.

Paolo Pace

Marc's nephew; the son of Marc's sister Colette

He was probably one of the most intensive pranksters ever. He was absolutely always looking for a way to get somebody. And sometimes—actually a lot of times, from what I've heard from his childhood—it got him into trouble. A lot. His father, my grandfather, was a navy captain for a greater portion of his career, and as I understand it he was in the navy for a total of 37 years. So this is a serious man. Quite a wonderful sense of humour in his own way but as a father I'm sure he was very strict. When Marc would do something such as play a prank you could imagine this big navy man coming down the hall to see what his son was up to.

He was the only son [in a family with] three daughters. So this was great for him in one sense, there was always someone around to play a trick on, but bad in the sense it was always easy to guess who had just made the sisters scream. So on one occasion, my mother—I think they were the closest in age, he used to play a lot of pranks on her—when it came time for bed he waited until my mother was in the bathroom washing up, brushing her teeth, and he snuck into her bedroom.

This prank was something that he'd planned out in phases. The first phase was that he went into the room, climbed underneath the bed, leaving the lights on so that everything would seem normal, and hid under there until she came in. She came in, she turned off the light, climbed into bed. He waited until her breath had regulated, until she was just fading into that first level of sleep, and then he reached out from underneath the bed and put a very rigid clawlike hand onto her and <u>scared</u> her. And of course she screamed, and in came my grandfather and grabbed him by the ear and hauled him out and gave him a talking-to. And of course he

1

waited very patiently, even though he knew he was going to get in trouble, he was very persistent at these things, he waited until the next evening and he crawled under the bed only this time he had his hand soaked in cold water.

Conceiving of this prank—at the same time he's persistent to come back, but [with] the ideas that were obviously changing through his head, he could spontaneously think of how the plan would be better. So he quickly jumps out and turns off the light and puts his [cold, wet] hand over the lightswitch. So as my mother comes in, not trusting at all, [thinking] he's probably in there and the lights are out, she cautiously puts her hand around the corner and starts feeling for the lightswitch until she comes across this cold, clammy hand that quickly grabs her. And so again she screams and down the hall comes my grandfather. I think he enjoyed the kind of attention he got which was obviously hinting at his future.

Another story—he was on the city bus with my mom when they were children and oftentimes he liked to, out of the blue, pretend that he didn't know my mother. But it wasn't so much acting nonchalant; as she would say something to him, he would become very offended. He'd say, "WHAT?! Ten <u>dollars</u>?! I will <u>not</u>! You're <u>disgusting</u>!" and he'd jump up and run to the other end of the bus. And everyone would look at my mother. Of course she's beet-red. She'd say "Marc! You know me! This isn't funny!" And he'd say "I don't know you and my name isn't Marc!" This was his kind of sense of humor. I was fortunate enough to get a taste of that too. At the time I was the only child in the family, so not only a single child but the only child, which made me prey. He saw new blood. Are you familiar with the movie "Liar Liar"? With Jim Carrey? There's a scene in that movie where he does something called The Claw to his son, where he gets this rigid hand and he attacks his son to tickle him. And when I saw that, that brought back great memories. I thought the only person who knew The Claw was my uncle Marc, because that's what he would do to me, he would come after me with The Claw and just tickle me until I couldn't stand it any more. Oftentimes my grandmother would chastise the both of us as if we were both children, which was always so fun but surprising too because I thought adults didn't get in trouble like that.

At dinnertime with that family, even adults became giddy with the thought of what he would be doing at the table that night. We never knew. He was the Robin Williams of our family. We'd sit down to dinner and even my grandfather would get this grin on his face and you just knew. We all expected something. He was just fantastic, ever the actor.

[Playing pranks on me] didn't require a whole lot of planning on his end. I could fall to pieces in laughter if he just looked at me funny from across the room. He'd make me weak. He'd sit in a chair across the room and he'd say, "I'm about to get up and I'm coming over there and I'm going to tickle you until you can't breathe anymore"; and I would want to get away but I'd be laughing so hard, I'd just fall into a pile of jelly on the spot. It was perfect. He never even had to get up.

He loved to play pranks on my mother a lot, but as she became more aware of his behavior, he decided rather than losing that sense of fun, he teamed up with my mom and then they'd just go after the youngest daughter. They would tell my aunt Denise, they'd suddenly jump out of bed and tell her not to move, the electric blanket was sparking.

I know that Marc was often very interested in the history of the family, always asking questions, and having my mother retell stories. The first Chabot to come across—this is something Marc used to like to hear, not in terms of how it was fun, but—the first member to come across to try to settle the new country was scalped and did not make it. So Mathurin Chabot, the next Chabot to come across, was indeed successful. A rather harsh way to get us across but we are here, thank goodness, but those were the harsh realities of the days back then.

3

Marc oftentimes—as I think it was with all of them—saw [travel] as a great opportunity to immerse himself in differences. To be a Canadian, and then to go to the U.S. which in itself can change from state to state, that's a difference. Here in Canada [we have] large provinces, so if you live in Ontario, the Ontario personality and mentality can be generalized until you cross the border into Quebec, where everything changes, whereas in the states there's a lot less distance to go to notice the differences. And then of course they traveled to Japan, a place he loved very much, there were differences there, and Australia—and everywhere they would go he would see these changes and these different people and attitudes and food.

So from what I remember is rather than that become a problem, it became almost a hobby, to go and to watch people and to see how they act and to just learn. It gave him a lot of perspective. It helped him.

He was the most forgiving person I've ever met. He had his days where he'd be upset, but not in a way I think you'd be prepared for. He was—in my interpretation, he was an angel. He was someone who could get angry but not make you feel shamed or embarrassed. He just had a way of saying, "You can't do that." He would speak this way, and even the harshest temper would be calmed right down. I'd like to think a lot of that came from the perspective he was given from travelling and seeing the difference in people.

I try and separate myself from my attachment to him to say I felt there was an immense amount of talent, just so much talent in one person. It was, from what I understand, from the stories and what I witnessed—a lot of it was natural. There was a natural charisma, a natural kind streak in him, a natural sense of happiness that is good if you want to entertain people. At the same time there was a drive, he worked very, very hard. You think about times where he was being given such credit for having such a wonderful voice, you'd think he would say "Oh, my voice is perfect, I

4

don't need to work on it." But he had a voice coach all along, always worked on his voice.

I hold a lot of my opinions and impressions from when I was a child, so that from the day that he left us it's as if I haven't really developed any new ideas. I still hold a lot of those childhood impressions in my head about him, but I was sad that I didn't get more of an opportunity to see him act, outside of the family fun.

I was sorry that I didn't get to see him get involved in projects that were maybe a little more mainstream. I know that he was not so much interested in the theatre after his time there because of the politics involved, the control issues you meet up with. I don't know if it would be any better if we were talking about Hollywood, but I'm just sorry he didn't get into a medium that might have exposed him to more people. Especially in terms of acting. Because acting is something that interests me personally and selfishly I would have loved to see him there, to have witnessed that part of him. I got to see him entertain thousands of people through song. I would have loved to see him entertain thousands of people through character.

It's sad to think something he had such a passion for could be blocked by maybe inhibitions, maybe people, but that's the part that shocks me most. Something I couldn't explain; I wish I could. This was a man who accepted people no matter what package they came in. If they were angry all the time, he was the person who looked beyond it. So even if you had an angry, foul person he softened them right up, he found the good in them. I found that shocking, [with] the passion he obviously had for acting he could walk away from that because of the people, just because of the atmosphere and what it did to people. I'm almost frightened to think of what he encountered. To take such a forgiving person and turn them to say "I'm sorry, this is not for me."

Surrounding the time after Marc passed there were a lot of very surreal, spiritual things that happened, not only witnessed by just me but witnessed by many people. Shortly

5

after he died we had the funeral, and the night before the funeral, Toronto experienced the most severe electrical storm that they had had in a long time. And his good, good friend Ian said at the funeral "I think he's trying out his new powers as an angel." That was his words at the funeral and everybody, it wasn't just this laughter, it was saying "Oh, you noticed it too!" This relief. Privately, you shyly admit to your close friends "You think? Maybe? You think that could be?" but I'm not surprised. It's very rare to have such great people. If you think about Marc, you're not thinking of Mr. Average. You're thinking about a truly unique and special person. If you believe in things as chi or a general spirit that connects us all, when someone as great as that, either known by millions or known by thousands or known by one, passes, I think it does affect the greater consciousness, people in general. That sadness travels from one person to the next which creates an environment, an atmosphere. Very strange but good things happened afterward that just made people realize, not only physically was he a special person but even after he passed he had a way of making your senses awaken to different possibilities, different ideas.

Chris Thomas

Marc's best friend at St. Patrick's, a Catholic boys' college preparatory high school in Ottawa.

I met Marc in the fall of 1962. He and his family had just moved from Halifax, Nova Scotia that summer. I don't know where they were living before Halifax, but they had lived in Ottawa before, I remember. The first day of school would have been the first time I met Marc. I don't know how long it took before we were friends. I don't remember being in high school and not being his friend. We would get together and sing Motown, you know, the Shirrelles, the Supremes, the Crystals.

Marc also listened to classical music a lot; his love of the classics rubbed off on me to some degree. Music was very important. He would go around singing snatches of song.

Fridays after school we'd leave at 3:10 and walk down Metcalf to downtown. My memories of high school are of walking up and down Metcalf endlessly with Marc. We were just two lonely, sensitive, intelligent misfits. We'd play chess, spend Saturday nights together, but we'd always spent Fridays together. At school, I and Marc were 1st and 2nd respectively. I'd have a 90-91%, Marc would be at about 84%. It didn't matter to him to be the top student. It was very important to me.

He began to act for Immaculata, a Catholic girl's high school, when they needed boys for the male roles in their plays. He acted, as I recall, in several of their plays. By Grade 11,12, 13 Marc was very popular with the girls. Oh, he was considered a real catch—I was not. I was four eyes, tall, thin and gangly. Marc was also a competitive swimmer; as I recall, he swam with a local swim-club.

One thing we had in common: Marc and I were very religious, he took his Catholic faith very seriously.

7

One time, he told me that, a few nights before, he had lain on the floor of his room with his ear-phones on and the music playing at full-blast. It seemed to me he was trying to drive something out of his mind.

In January 1967, he did what today we would call "coming out" to me on a very cold Friday night, on one of our interminable walks through older parts of Ottawa. We had gone out together for the evening, as we always did. He said to me, "Remember that Sunday afternoon last fall when I was supposed to come over and play chess? Well, I met a man at the bus stop who invited me to come home with him. And that's what I did. I've decided that I am a homosexual." I admitted to him that I had a fascination with boys, even the word "boy" was exciting, interesting to me. But I couldn't do then what he did, to say, "I've decided that I am a homosexual."

It is essential to realize the narrowness of the environment in which we grew up. There was sophistication in Ottawa, Canada's capital, but it was at higher levels than ours, connected to the government. I didn't even realize that—the "other" Ottawa. The Ottawa that we grew up in, in the early to mid-'60s, was not the mid-sized, cosmopolitan city it is now. Our Ottawa was tremendously isolated and provincial; stodgy, conservative, backward. To have anything to eat after 10 o'clock, you had only one place where you could go, the Party Palace Deli on Elgin. I wanted to get out to Toronto as soon as possible. In such an environment [as Ottawa], we hardly had words for our experience of not fitting in. It is very much to Marc's credit, I now see, that he admitted his sexual orientation as early as he did (age 17 or 18) in that hostile environment. At the time, I thought he was going to hell.

Marc was very close to his mother [Yolande]. He probably was able to "tell her" quite early on, only shortly after [telling] me. She was very sympathetic to and supportive of him. She was a real source of strength to him, and now...I think that's why I liked being around his home as much as I did.

Marc's relationship with his father, Tom Connors, was different. I recall him as severe looking, he seldom smiled—but I don't think he was as severe as Marc thought he was. Outsiders could see a quiet, dour charm in Tom. He could be pretty hard on his son. Marc was very close to his mother, not so close to his father—classic pattern, really, for a gay boy. As I got older, I came to respect and rather like Tom. Of course, he was not my dad, and I think to a degree I played up to him just to win one-up on Marc. But I also came to see that, beneath his gruff officer's exterior was a truly witty and wonderful man. I hope Marc came to see that, too—I believe he did. Marc came of <u>very</u> good people, and I'm honoured to have known them.

Yolande I consider a woman of great style and humour, charming, vivacious; she treated me splendidly. She and Marc together played a practical joke on me one time—I had been fascinated by an ornate dish of theirs, it was a blue glass bowl which rested in a silver, filigreed outer dish. I turned it over to see the maker's name and the inner glass bowl fell to the floor and broke. Marc and his mother treated the incident very seriously, said it was very expensive and I had to pay for it, find a replacement. I felt like two cents looking for change.

This went on for quite some time, I was calling all over looking for a replacement, but finally they told me it really wasn't a big deal–they had been joking all the time, at the expense of my sensitivity. So, you see, Marc and his mother, together, could make quite a devastating team.

Another joke. I remember Marc visiting me at my home one Friday afternoon, after school. We were alone in the house. Marc was kidding around, and I remember him clambering up on the back of our sofa and getting into pounce position, like the incubus. "I am Yama, the God of Death," he intoned fearsomely. He was a great entertainer from the start. I remember some utterly uproarious times

9

together. I don't think I have laughed like that since, right from the belly.

Being religious and Catholic (and not very attracted to girls) in that time, it was natural for us to think about becoming priests, and in the summer of 1963 we took what was called a "vocational workshop" at the Oblate scholasticate east of Ottawa, on the Montreal road. The young Oblate scholastics ran a sort of summer camp for a week, the purpose of which was to help Catholic boys decide if they wanted to be priests. Marc went one summer, not again; I went to several. I think Marc did not like it. He was more rebellious than I. For both of us, it was an immature idea to become a priest, born of a childlike devotion we both had.

Again, it's important to realize that those years were stormy not only for us, but for the whole Catholic Church. It was a kind of collective adolescence. This was exactly the period of the Second Vatican Council. The Church was changing almost weekly, and it was hard to know where anything stood. We had religion classes at school, but toward the end, when we were in grades 11-13, there was a real effort made to make them relevant to our experience. I remember, in particular, one priest—he is still an Oblate, and a damned good one—taught us sex education; the class, naturally, was uproarious, but to this day I have the greatest respect for the priest who saw our need and took it on and let us have our own responses. Marc eventually broke with the Church, when he was 18 or so, much, I suspect, to his mother's chagrin.

Incidentally, in Grade 13, when we were 18, our class went on a two-day retreat at the retreat house, also east of Ottawa. It was given by a handsome young priest, whose name I forget but who was involved in religious broadcasting. Marc fell madly in love with him, and I recall our going to visit him together once or twice.

As some of the things I've said suggest, Marc and I were very competitive. For a year or two, we would get together

10

and play chess on the weekends—Friday nights, Sunday afternoons. Marc was a much better chess-player than I and consistently beat me. One evening, I got so furious with him I literally threw him out of the house and told him to go home. Seeing him there, shivering on the front step in Ottawa's winter, I thought better of myself and invited him back in and apologized. But it was a measure of how threatened I felt by Marc's evident success. We had a summer job together for a week or two one year, at St. Pat's, repairing textbooks, fixing hundreds of books. I remember running up and down the tops of desks, these old-fashioned desks that were bolted to the floor, you know. I remember one time I got so angry with him that I punched out a glass panel door. I still have the scar...

He also had a particularly annoying gesture, which he knew "bugged" me and he used it to the hilt: he would rub his thumb and finger up and down the sides of his nose with complete, glacial sang-froid—it gave him a very arch look. Marc could be quite cool and arrogant, and unfortunately that's the side I saw of him more than any other in later life. Marc and I began to grow apart after Grade 13. It was partly his frank acknowledgment of his sexuality and partly a matter of growing apart in interests.

After Grade 13, we went together to Glendon College of York University. As I said, I had been determined to go to Toronto, and I think Marc and I had this romantic attachment to the idea of the English college. We went to look at the place for a few days during our senior (Grade 13) year. Incidentally, on that or another trip I remember Marc becoming thoroughly depressed at the appearance of Toronto. Driving in on Highway 402, over the rooftops of Agincourt, with their sea of TV antennas, Marc got very upset at the impersonality of it all.

At Glendon, the two of us were the top students in English in the whole college. This is quite a tribute to Oblate Father Gus McKinnon, who had taught us English. (Gus' classes appeared totally directionless, a joke, but in fact he

11

taught us so much through discussion and apparently random reflections. In the end, he was a brilliant teacher, and we were lucky to have him.)

Marc became involved in amateur drama productions put on in the "Pipe Room," a sort of coffeehouse—this was 1967!—in Glendon Hall. Marc spent just the one year— 1967-8—at Glendon, then left and started the drama program in Alberta.

In November 1971, while Marc was still at Alberta and I was doing a stint as a church volunteer in northern British Columbia, I visited Edmonton and stayed with him. My clearest memory is of sharing a futon with him and waking up in the middle of the night to find his arm across me. I was terrified. (Trust me: Homophobia knoweth no bounds!) I saw him little after that, in Edmonton, while he was on the road, and during the Stratford period.

After he and Paul, Arnold, and the others started The Nylons, I took a sort of interest in him again. I simply loved the music! Once a year or so, I would go to a Nylons concert, meet Marc, and perhaps go to dinner with him after.

It is a shame we were not closer. Today I would call him up and say, "Let's get together, we need to talk." I'd take him out for dinner and we would talk, there'd be so much to say. But I was diffident and I did not do that. He was soaring and I was jealous.

I came quite to dislike him, partly out of jealousy for the success of his career, to which what appeared to me the disarray of my own compared unfavourably. Also, as I reflect on it...Marc did not quite know how to be around me. We grew apart; he saw that I was fighting my own sexuality, and, frankly, he just didn't know how to relate to me. So, I suspect, he put on a façade of coolness and indifference, which was not really "him". I feel very much at peace with him now and sometimes find myself talking to him in the spirit. He was, in a way, the best friend I ever had.

Jo Leslie

A friend of Marc's from his theatre days in Toronto

How did you meet Marc?

That's my favorite part. Everything else—I was just trying to make some notes beforehand and I wasn't coming up with a lot of concrete stuff, it was just edges of memories here and there. I had recently moved to Toronto and had just turned 18 and was cast in a production of the Tempest. I knew the director [Cheryl Cashman], and she'd cast me in it. I was gonna be Ariel's sidekick. I had a non-speaking role where I would prance around and do magic with Ariel. Marc was Ariel, and that's how we met, we were cast in this play together.

I was totally smitten on the spot with this Greek Adonis-looking man who moved beautifully too. We went in the studio and rehearsed together to try and find out some kind of vocabulary, because it wasn't a written part that I had, so we were just making it up. He was very very structured and I wasn't. He really liked to order everything. He was always kind of like had an older brother attitude toward me even though I was always in love with him. But anyway…that's how we met. I guess not quickly enough for him but quickly enough it became clear that we'd never get together as I'd hoped but it turned into this wonderful friendship that lasted until he died. We became very very dear close friends. But strangely enough I can't remember a lot of details within that. We were roommates several times, and we just kept showing up in each other's lives at different points.

[In this Tempest] I just went around and cast spells on people, I helped do Prospero's magic, basically sort of pranced about behind Marc. I remember him perched way up on the pulpit. It was a very big church, and we were

13

gonna use the big open area, and for some reason they decided it was just too open and they wanted to enclose it to give the sense of this island that they were on. So we did it in the sanctuary. It was incredibly intimate, I would say crowded, and Marc was—actually there was a wonderful picture in the publicity of that of Marc perching up on the pulpit.

He was very very light. Had a dancer's body really. Beautiful long arms and legs, and long neck. He always used his physicality to advantage [like when] he was tearing off his shirt in one of those James Dean-type moments of The Nylons' performances, he did that a few times. And he just loooved it. People would scream and he would just loooove it! He was such a performer, he was such, such a performer. The thing about him as a person, as a performer, was his generosity. He loved to give to people, and share with people, and be involved with people. He was like that in his personal life and he was like that onstage too.

He was always giving gifts, he loved to give gifts and make meals for people and welcome people into his home. The kitchen and cooking was always a big, big part of his life, coming over for a meal or there would be a good stew on the stove—it was just part of that sense of living with a sense of generosity.

[His cooking was] why I got him on board at the Queen Mother, which would be skipping ahead a few years. Before that we shared an apartment down on Queen Street in Toronto when there was nothing, nothing there, and we were roommates. I can't remember exactly what he was doing at that time, but I remember one musical that he was in, that he was really great in, Harry's Back in Town. It was in an uptown theatre, with Marty Short.

That was much more his style. I was doing a lot of the experimental theatre with Cheryl. There was one show that we did together, with Cheryl, Ian, Marc, me and a few other people who'd work off and on with Cheryl over the years called "Where's the Voice Coming From?" It was written

14

by Rudy Weeb. We did that at Factory Lab. I think that was somewhere around '77.

What was that play about?

Oh God. See, the other problem in those days was that, even though I kept being used in these theatre pieces, I was much more a dancer, that was my training. And I didn't pay a lot of attention, it's really bad to say, but, anyway, now I teach at the National Theatre School of Canada, so that's all been changed. In those days, I just sort of went along, you know? "Let's collaborate." "Oh, sure, let's collaborate." Whatever. (laughs)

The work was all very collaborative. I did a show with [Cheryl] on the Group of Seven—it was called Landscapes, and the cast put it together ourselves, we researched together and then we put together skits and ideas and images and songs, because Cheryl would always work with people who had all these different abilities to bring in. Marc wasn't in that one.

And then we did another one called Allen Gardens, which was based on a public gardens that was mostly homeless people and street people. We just went and hung out there for three weeks and basically wrote down our conversations and experiences and good character sketches and created a theatre piece from it. We did a sequel to it, on the city. We just basically went out everywhere and did the same process, came back with scenes of things—I remember specifically we did a whole thing on bars in Toronto and all these conversations and scenes that we witnessed there and put it together. I can't quite remember if Marc was in that or not...I have a feeling he might have been. These are the kinds of shows that Cheryl was doing. But Marc wasn't— although he was a good friend of Cheryl's, because they had been at university, the U of A at the same time, it wasn't really his thing.

15

[His was] a much more stylized kind of theatre, formal type of theatre. He had such a presence too. To put him in one of those little intimate performances that we did, it would blast everybody out of the hall. He needed big venues. I don't know if that's how he felt at the time but looking back I can see why it didn't really work.

But the thing also that I remember about Marc was that he was always investigating things, he was always reading up on new techniques of meditation, techniques of bodywork, of diet, he was really invested in self-improvement, in a very focused way. He always did a lot of reading—oh, he'd just read this thing about such and such a juice and he's gonna start juicing now. Or this kind of food or this kind of thing.

He introduced me to the Alexander technique, actually. It was developed by R.H. Alexander who was an actor who had vocal problems, and he tried to figure out why, and he discovered that it had to do with alignment, relationship of the spine with the head. And so from that he developed a way of working with the body to help people work with a natural alignment that would not only help actors but help people generally to have a more efficient body use. It's based a lot on how children are naturally aligned too.

Anyway, Marc was quite into that. But he would like really go into these different things and pull material out that he could apply to himself and his own purposes, in his own discipline and also in his own daily life too. There was always something that he was into. But it was interesting, because I'd always learn things. 'Cause he was always learning things. He really had an appetite for being informed. Anything towards health and betterment of self and self-growth.

At one point, as fate would have it, I had moved out to Vancouver in '80 to work with a dance company there, and Marc showed up. The Nylons were there for a month in Vancouver. I ended up getting kicked out of the apartment that I was in and once again Marc said "Come and stay with me!" So once again we were together and while we were together there the Alvin Ailey Company came into town. And I had studied with them in New York, and was friends with a couple of them. And so Marc and I went to see the Ailey Company together and we went backstage to see [my friend], Milton.

It was his birthday and it was the day or two before Marc's birthday as well so we all went out and we just spent this incredibly magical night together...I mean, The Nylons and the Ailey Company! It was just great. And the Ailey Company were there for at least a week or more for some reason as well, so we got both companies together and it was just an incredible high, love-in, these amazing talents all brought together. Stuff like that was always happening. Very, very creative.

Going back to the beginning of The Nylons coming out of the Queen Mother, like I say I was there at the beginning, my boyfriend at that time opened the Queen Mother. He was a lawyer and had no restaurant experience. I had been waitressing like most dancers for years already, and I said, "Well, you gotta do this, gotta do this, gotta do this," whatever. So I was the first waitress there and was kinda like co-running the place. Even before it opened, he said, "We need cooks" and I said, "Marc and Ian are fabulous cooks, they're always into all this, they're really into recipe books and doing it right." They were vegetarian at the time, and we wanted to have vegetarian stuff in the restaurant. So I remember introducing Marc and Andre to each other and Marc coming over with his recipes prepared, [he was] always really prepared. So I said, "Okay, let's do it." And so the first menu was basically Marc and Ian's concoction. There they were in the kitchen and there I was serving, I mean, it was hysterical. But we had a ball.

And then from that, and then Denis Simpson, who you must have heard of, who was an original member who was a pal of mine and Marc's also, a wonderfully talented actor and singer, he was two doors over in a musical revue/cabaret

17

kind of thing, he'd come over at closing time, these guys get together at closing time and they just start singing. And then they went over to Paul's, and they would literally go up on the roof and sing. That's how the whole thing got going. When the Queen Mother first opened, it was this tiny sliver of a restaurant, we moved tables and chairs away and the guys sang.

And then they sang at a lot of parties. Loft parties were really big then. Lots of people lived in lofts at that point, and they would have these big parties where like a hundred people would come. And so there was this perfect venue for The Nylons to start to have an audience. There was probably no money involved, but they would just show up and sing and people would like what they heard. And I remember their first public performance outside of that was in this ice cream restaurant place in Yorkville [Scoops]. An ice cream restaurant! I don't know what they were doing there!

I'm so grateful that I was a part of [that Toronto scene]. Just so much was cooking in theatre and dance, it was a very exciting time. And the Queen Mother became a real focal point within that, within the art community. I got so much work just from waitressing there, the people coming in and saying, "Hey, Jo, I'm doing this project, are you interested?" There was just so much contact—networking I guess is the word—that went on. I'm trying to remember, things moved so fast for The Nylons after that, suddenly then I'm remembering their manager, and his girlfriend Susan was a dancer, and then I remember them doing this performance in front of Bette Midler, at the Toronto Film Festival. And that was really early on.

This limo came and picked us up, and they had this terrible performance because the mikes weren't working. And it was just—Oh, my God! They were just like peeing in their pants. Because they had been so worked up, 'cause she was a big icon for the boys, you know? And they were just wilting, they were right in front of her table. And the sound was hideous. So that was really tough. But then things just

18

seemed to—phrooooshhh (sound of a rocket ship)—just take off from there. I counted about eight apartments that I remembered Marc and Ian having. But I can't necessarily remember the order of them or the dates, but they moved so many times. There were so many parties and so many places all the time.

Like I say, I can't quite put it all together, because I've got this one memory of one place and then suddenly, whoop, it's another place. But that was the same thing for me in those days. I never lived anywhere more than, certainly not as long as a year, in any one place. Everybody seemed to— there were a lot of shared houses, and then for whatever reason people would get out and try something else or whatever.

I remember also going back [to Vancouver] in '82, pregnant, and Paul Cooper telling me the story of his birth on a table in a kitchen in Texas and he was twenty pounds. Like all Paul Cooper's stories! The guys were just flying in those days. Except for—Marc had recurrent throat problems. I think that was later though, that that really became a real problem for him. Again, he was constantly trying different things and trying to find a way to relieve that. And then of course in the later years there was a lot of conflict between him and Paul. Things really going sour there. By that time I was in Montreal and it was much more sporadic when I was seeing Marc.

But they were often in Vancouver and so was I, in the summers. So I had a number of visits with him out there. And I would keep in touch. Up to about the mid-eighties, I really kept quite a bit in touch with Toronto, and would go back there. And then I saw Marc here in 90, they opened for the Bee Gees at the Forum. And there was a big review in the paper on my solo show, and [Marc] had seen it on the plane on the way in, and he was just like, "Oh, I'm so happy for you, I'm so proud!" But that was the thing, it was always this big brother kind of thing, "I'm so proud of you, I'm so proud of you!" And we had a visit that day, and then there was the show and then they were off.

But we kept in touch with each other. He was a very loyal friend that way. I think he was very much that way with his family too. He would always talk to me about his sisters, and keep me up to date on his sisters, and would like me to meet them, he said, "Oh, my sisters are gonna be there tonight, I want you to meet them." They were really important to him as well. As much as he was gay he loved having women around him. Even though he was the star pretty much we just had as playful a time as ever with him. He was still always Marc. He didn't change with all of that at all. He adored teasing me and that never ended. I guess 'cause he had all these sisters that he grew up with. He was the only boy, so...Oh, he'd, um—well, I had a bump on my head, that you couldn't see, but he'd always call me Ol' Bumpy, he's the only person who ever called me that in my entire life. But he'd rub my head a lot, and call me Ol' Bumpy. And then I would always go on about my weight, whether it was going up or down, being a dancer, and at a certain point it really had gone up, and he would sing the "Teddy Bears' Picnic" to me in a particular [low] tone...But he just loved joking around, he loved it. He was a tease with everybody actually.

Sometimes he would get me a bit pissed, but it wasn't a big deal. It was all in fun. He was very, almost protective of me actually, like wanted to make sure I was taken care of. I probably had a waifish aspect to my nature. But that was his way of showing his love, really. He was very, very caring.

[Things between Marc and Paul] became very hostile. But you see, I wasn't around during it so I would just get spurts of stuff about it. But Marc was just...devastated, broken up by it. Whatever had gone down, I guess it became a power issue, that was my sense of it, I don't know. I don't know all the ins and outs of it. There seemed to be a lot of conflict around Peter Mann, who Marc just adored, and around arrangements and who was singing leads. It really

20

was so hard—the only thing that stands out in my mind was I'd never seen Marc so crushed by something, and not knowing where to go or how to figure this thing out, whether to—I mean, he was gonna quit, he was gonna quit The Nylons. It was getting to that. And I guess it never really got resolved.

And I don't know what the timing of that and the start of [Marc's] illness was either. His illness certainly went quickly. But—I went over to his place, and—I can't remember a lot about that too, about knowing that he was sick. I went, and I was so startled by how changed his appearance was. And he was wearing makeup and—but, he was teasing me. And goofing around, he had Ian take some pictures of us together, and that was great. Actually, I'm mixing that up with another time at the same house, we had Ian taking some pictures of us, and he was kicking his legs up in the air and laughing and giggling and being geeky. But even still, when he was sick, and I went there, and he was so physically changed, you know, we went out to a store together. He was continuing, to perform, and I just thought, "Oh, my God! The courage!" The absolute courage, that he would just keep on. It was just amazing.

How did you find out he was sick?

I can't quite pinpoint that. That's what I can't put together, because in '90 I saw him here at the Forum, and he wasn't sick, or he wasn't showing it or maybe he told me then or something. But I'm trying to remember when it was that I actually had that visit in Toronto when I saw him and he was quite changed. I guess it must have been in the fall of '90 or something like that. But I must have known that Ian had been sick first, you see? I knew about that. Then I guess Marc must have told me. I am sure I blocked that from my mind, finding that out. It would take a lot to call that up, I think. No, I don't really know how I found out. But I remember very clearly when Ian called me to tell me he had died and I was in absolute disbelief. But at the same

21

time my legs buckled, and I went down on the floor. It was so shocking. Because actually I had received a postcard from Marc the week before from Arizona, saying when he was gonna be back. Telling me when he was gonna be back so we could see each other. I had just got that a week before he died. That was something, he did write, he sent postcards from different places that he was. He definitely kept in touch.

What do you remember about how the whole group got along?

To begin with, Denis and Marc were real buddies, real good friends. Denis and I are still in touch, not as much as I'd like to be. And then Ralph came in and joined in. Ralph was really wonderful. But then Ralph left, it wasn't what he wanted to be doing. Then they asked Denis to come back, but Denis didn't want to. And then Arnold joined. I got the sense they were [all friends]. I'm talking about the early years though. They were just doing this cool thing, and this thing that they totally got off on, and people were loving it! That's the thing, they were going, "People are going nuts over this! Oh, my God, this is great!"

And for Marc, he really took it as a theatrical performance, too. He would try to bring a theatricality and choreography into each song, an interpretation for each song. He loved that. That song where he ripped his shirt open, I just remember the look on his face. He was so over the moon with happiness that such a corny thing would get everybody going. He just <u>had</u> everybody. He wasn't taking himself seriously with it. He was just having a ball with that, it was a Gene Pitney song, and he'd strike this Gene Pitney pose. But they loved doing that, like way, way later, the "Chain Gang" choreography that they did with the mikes. [*For "Chain Gang," The Nylons would throw their mikestands over their shoulders and shuffle around the stage as though they were convicts hauling heavy sacks.*] That was a lot of his inventiveness. That was one thing that bothered

22

him about Paul. Paul had a lot of rhythm, but because of his size, he wasn't a very agile mover. Marc loved putting in these flairs, he had so much flair as a performer. Style I guess would be the better word. And Claude had dance background too. Certainly Denis was a dancer. So when Denis was in there, they had fun with those things. Every song they tried to create a whole atmosphere with, with the lighting, with the choreography, with the characterization they would put into it.

[Like] Lion Sleeps Tonight, the whole jungle thing that they did. They were always developing it, all of the sounds of the jungle, having the theatre almost dark at the beginning, and having all the sounds and then gradually gradually leading into the song and then him and Claude would do this physical back and forth thing to mirror the vocals. He just adored that. It wasn't just the singing, it was the whole visual, theatrical presentation of each song. That was really important.

Then they'd bring in new songs, and then they would start writing too. I have this really clear memory of walking up Spadina Avenue and Marc singing me the lyrics of Prince of Darkness that he'd just written, before it went in to be arranged and recorded or whatever. They started to not only arrange other people's material, but then to start developing their own material. So it was this constant font of creativity. Just trying to find different ways to entertain. Marc was also a very, conscientious individual—he had a very spiritual sense of who he was and of purpose and that was behind a lot [of his actions]. As much as he just loved to entertain people, he liked to be able to put in his own messages— certainly Prince of Darkness was one of [those message songs]. He saw what an incredible vehicle [songwriting] was for his own voice. So he started to use that.

What did you think about these message songs?

It was a discussion we would have because it was the times, we were all into spiritual endeavors of different kinds and looking into different things. We'd talk about how we could use it to inform our work. Marc could reach such huge audiences. My work was much more fringe kind of stuff. He felt that within something being entertaining it could also carry a message. He was very proud of his songs. You can feel the power of them when he was performing them. That was something that was important to him. It was interesting to see the progression of that, to go from "Gee this is fun" to "Oh, my God, this is taking off. Whoa, this is going somewhere we never anticipated," to "Okay, now then, how can I actually use this to bring something through of my own personal vision?"

Marc, underneath all that light and fun, wasn't. He was a very serious individual. He took what he did very very seriously. He took his friendships seriously, he took his work very, very seriously. That's why I say when he came to meet my boyfriend Andre talking about the restaurant, he came with his recipes. That's just so much how he was. When he started to have those throat problems, that became such a difficult thing for him. He was doing this Chinese tea stuff, all these different things to try and make it go away. Marc was adamant about training, his physical training and his vocal training. He saw a voice coach, and he worked with specialists on his throat problems when he started to have them. Because he wanted to develop as much as stay in shape for what he was doing. He wanted to just get better so he could do more things.

Because Marc had very high expectations of himself and very high aspirations, it was incredibly disheartening when other people didn't keep up with that. Actually I think that's somewhere where Marc and I met, in a way, there was this sense of purpose and of bringing a personal vision through into the work so it is art (for him) as much as entertainment. I've never gone towards entertainment myself. That's a lot

24

of how we talked about stuff, he didn't really talk to me a lot about the business—different arrangements. Actually, I went into the studio a few times with them in Toronto in the earlier days, when Peter Mann first started working with them. Just hearing them, listening to cuts.

Everybody was there the day I went in. I was really like one of the gang, 'cause I was there from the beginning, I was there from before the beginning. I wasn't a groupie because I was a personal friend, but I was always around with the guys and I was always warmly welcomed by them all. And even like the last show that I saw, which I just couldn't…it was not long after Marc died, I mean really not long at all and they performed at the Spectrum in Montreal. Ian was there and I went and I just bawled my eyes out. It was too hard. But I went backstage afterwards and [saw] it was really hard for them too, oh they were a mess afterwards. I think it was like a month or so [afterward]. But that's the last time I saw them actually. Claude's still there, isn't he? Amazing. And Arnold? Oh my God. I heard them on the radio not long ago and I thought, "Oh my God!" This is like 20 years later. 'Cause I remember the day, I don't know why, we were in the Eaton Centre, this big brand-new shopping centre in Toronto and I was in this small theatre [piece] we were doing it in the middle of the Eaton Centre. And the guys were there—Marc and I guess maybe Denis—we were hanging around and they said, "We found our fourth member," and it was Claude. They said "But he's in hospital. But we went in and we said, 'Claude, you're the fourth member.'" And I just remember being in this shopping centre, hanging over a railing on the third floor with the guys telling me like "There's this falsetto guy, but he's in hospital, but he'll be out soon and so we can get started." For some reason that's a really clear memory.

But I was there a lot with them, well of course Marc didn't last long in the restaurant, but Ian stayed on longer. I was always coming and going—I left and came back a couple of times. But like I say when I went out to

Vancouver, then the next thing you know The Nylons showed up there. That was in '80 and already things were happening for them.

What about your relationship with Marc? You said you fell hard for him—did that present any difficulties?

The thing [about how I felt about him] was it took me a little bit longer than it should have probably to get it clear what the picture was here, you know? Like, get over it, he's not gonna change. But we were kind of in love—we were in love with each other, and that's why our friendship was as strong as it was. Because, we were so close, it's just that we didn't sleep together—well, actually, we did sleep together, but we didn't make love! So, we were that close, there was an incredible amount of love between us, which I'm forever grateful for.

Marc was such a bright light in my life. He was so positive, and I was going here and there and doing all these different things but I could always go and talk it through with Marc, whatever was going on, he would always be right there. I think when you know people before they get famous or whatever it's like that. I don't know how much people really change. For me, I don't take it like "Oh, my God, you're somebody different now." I was one of the gang. I was actually more than that to Marc, we were very very dear friends, there was no question. It was nice to spend time talking about him.

I know one thing about Marc in terms of his character was that his mum was Quebecois, and I think a lot of his sense of—I'm married to a Quebecois, so I can say this!—a lot of his sense of warmth, of the home, of cooking, all of that kind of thing I think was very much from his mum, and that he had a really hard time with his dad, who was military. That Marc was gay and an artist and all of that, I think that was really, really difficult. He was able to celebrate so much his feminine aspect without losing the male. I could really see that in his character.

26

Also his face, he looked so—it's such a classical face, it's from another time or something. Which he used. He used everything to great advantage. He worked everybody, that guy. He would schmooze. "Oh look, there's an important-looking person, let's go find out who that is." We just had so much fun that way.

What I found so remarkable in that last year [was] that he continued performing even though his looks had changed so much. I just found that phenomenal, phenomenal, phenomenal. I can't even put words around what that did to me to know that...what it must have taken out of him to be up and down planes. He talked about that at a certain point; he said, "I am just exhausted." But he kept going. I don't think I've thought about it too much 'cause I don't want to, how that illness just like phheeww, swept him away so quickly. But there was something about this whole thing with Paul, too, that his spirit was broken over that, I had never ever ever seen him like that. So, I don't know if we'll ever know the ins and outs of...Well, if I ever run into Paul Cooper, I will ask him. And it might help him to just clear it too, 'cause he knows how close Marc and I were.

Anyway, I miss those days. We had such a great time. Such such such a great time—and the thing was that as much as Marc was incredibly meticulous and really thought so much about each song, each note, each "what's this mean? How can we get this [to be] a better idea?"—there was so much play involved also. And that was so much a part of his creativity too. That's what I saw, when this whole thing was happening with Paul, it was like his spirit was really broken, like there was no play left anymore. It was awful. Even more than about him getting sick! Maybe that's the thing, maybe his spirit had already been broken and...I don't know. One can only speculate.

Oh, yeah, that's another thing. Ian put together a tribute performance to Richard and Marc and I performed at that in Toronto. And it was incredible. Andre, my boyfriend who'd started the Queen Mother, then opened up another restaurant (he's gone on to be this unbelievably successful restauranteur, opening his fourth restaurant) and the second one that he opened—the Queen Mum has expanded three times, and is still a thriving place, it's a whole legend, it's a whole part of the legend, the Queen Mother and The Nylons. But anyway, Andre opened this other restaurant that has a club in the back of it, and Ian put together this tribute to Richard and Marc there. He had their pictures on the walls and he had his own artwork. He'd done a lot of silkscreen and batiking and painting, and had this stuff all over the walls. All kinds of different things about the two of them and then people who had been close to them performed.

There was myself, Linda Mancini, Ian—his clown was called Nion—did something, and I can't remember who else performed. I did an excerpt of my work called "Living in a Dangerous Time" which was about, well, it wasn't about AIDS, it was about death, and it was about a journey through death and transformation. Anyway, I performed it there. I always would change the ending depending on where I was performing. This was incredible. It was this tiny little stage that was meant for bands, right? With this disgusting carpet that stank of beer and cigarettes. And this really low ceiling. This tiny little space, and then this catwalk, and so, like I say, the piece is about death and transformation, and then at the end, I'd been using this huge piece of fabric and using it in different ways. I had put it down at one point and then danced very dramatically—it was all very dark and dramatic. And then at the end I would go and pick up the fabric and I would leave. It was this whole thing about leaving, when you leave.

Anyway, my fabric had ended up down at the end of the catwalk. I had decided that I would just go down the stairs off the catwalk and just exit through the space. Well, the place was packed to the rafters, literally people were sitting up on the bar to watch the performance, they were everywhere, it was packed packed packed. I picked up this fabric and there was no room for me to get down off the

28

stage. The only thing I could do was to get down by almost climbing onto people to get down and then to walk through this crowd of mostly gay men by—I had to touch everybody to move them, to get through. And everybody was crying. I was just walking and touching everybody, and I guess Marc was there and Richard was there, connection was being made. It was one of the most powerful experiences I've ever had with an audience. It was just incredible. That was our way of saying thank you and goodbye to our friends. I'm so thankful that Ian put that together. I guess it was shortly after that that he left.

I was in Vancouver about three or four years ago, I was only there for two days and I spent one day with Ian—and he said then that he'd only just been able to start listening to Marc's music again. It had been four or five years since he died. They were together forever those guys. And they had a cat called George who lived with them all the time and no matter how many different apartments they were in, George was always there, I have to tell you that. George was a big part of their life. And actually, now, what happened with that? Oh—George died around the time that Marc did. I don't know who went first.

Paul Cooper

A founding member of The Nylons; he and Marc sang most of the leads.

I originally met Marc when I lived in an apartment on Gerard. I saw him on the next balcony over and we started chatting. That was the summer of 1977. We were all doing musical theatre—I had met Denis [Simpson] about the same time, through mutual friends, running into each other at auditions.

Claude was doing "Kiss Me Kate" in London [Ontario] and we went to see another friend in the show. They were in a blackout; they had lost power that night. The whole cast was in the dressing room, somebody had an electric guitar, and everybody was singing songs. I heard this incredible, high voice. Later Marc and myself, we had been just singing, I happened to mention to Marc, "I met this guy, he's got a really great high tenor voice." So I was the one who introduced Marc and Claude. It all happened around summer and fall of '77 for Marc, summer of '78 for Claude and then by '79 we were performing.

A friend had a cafe up in Yorkville. Every Thursday they had a sing for your supper. We knew 4 songs. We thought, "We're out of work"—between engagements, you know—"We'll sing these four songs." It was February 20, 1979—I remember because that was my birthday. We said, "It's a one shot deal, we'll call ourselves 'The Nylons'." They made us do all four songs again!

The problem was Denis was already in a most successful show, "Indigo." It was the longest running show in Toronto at the time. So we had to work around his schedule, do a midnight appearance here, there, at a fashion show. This was no pay—we just did it out of love. Eventually we were doing a party at my house and this friend of ours who was starting a club, he said, "You can work at my club if you can fill out a whole act." So we had to say, "Denis, we have an offer for a real gig..." At that time, there was big talk of him going to Broadway with this show.

I had worked with Ralph [Cole] quite a few years before that in children's theatre. We were really theatrically based then; I knew that Ralph had the training, he could dance and move. I told the other guys, "You don't know this guy, but he'd be great." So we phoned him up—he was in Vancouver—and I told him, "We've got this group. You don't know any of these guys, but trust me. Come to Toronto." So he got on a plane and flew out!

When Ralph Cole left the group, how did you find Arnold Robinson?

Arnold auditioned for us. We did an extensive search for a bass singer. I always said tenors are a dime a dozen— to find a voice like Claude's, to find a voice like Arnold's, that's the hard part. One of the co-producers of Indigo had known Arnold; he told him, "There's this group and you should check it out."

He had stopped performing. He hadn't performed in a while. But we had gigs, y'know, we could offer him a real job. Shortly after that we put out the record, and that's when we really started to take off.

Peter Mann is the arranger for a great number of Nylons songs. How did you come to work with him?

I had known Peter [Mann] years and years. Years ago, '69, '70 was when I first met Peter, he was in a band called Sugar Shop—he was the singer, leader, and arranger. I was a roommate with Victor Garber—he was just in "Titanic"—I met Peter through Victor. Coincidentally, Marc had worked with Peter in a show called "Harry's Back in Town." Marty Short was in it—The Nylons used to rehearse at Second City's Firehall. The whole troupe would stop and run down, totally disrupt rehearsals. He's a great friend, Marty—and so was Gilda, they were so into what we were doing. They'd run downstairs and say, "Can we just listen?"

Marc had worked with Peter and I knew Peter. He wasn't even interested in working with us, he didn't even know what a cappella was really, it was just barbershop, he thought. Marc kept going to him and saying, "Paul Cooper's in this band, I'm in this band, won't you work with us?"— basically coerced him! Then he realized right away there was something going on here. I can't remember—did he work on our first album? I don't think so. I think he came on at <u>One Size Fits All</u>.

The first album, we put that together all by ourselves. Did all the arrangements, of course we wrote the original material. We had the record before we had a record contract. It was a great bargaining tool with the record companies. They didn't have to put out any initial money—making a debut album is a huge risk for a record company, and with what we were doing, everybody was like, "No way." It wasn't like what other people were doing, it wasn't punk rock. But we had a huge following. The record company knew it wasn't going to cost them anything to make the album 'cause we had enough of an audience, we could just sell it at our shows and there wouldn't be any loss. Our record went gold in a few weeks. It was kind of a shock for us!

Greg Stevenson was our original manager, and shortly after that Greg teamed with Wayne Thompson who had done a lot of things in music. They shopped it to Attic. Attic was at the time if it isn't still the only major independent label in Canada. Again, one of the execs was a big fan—Tom Williams, he was the one, and Al Mair, they were the two people who owned Attic basically. Mair had money, Williams was the artistic one. He brought us in.

32

What was it like in the studio?

We used every technique we knew and we invented a bunch. We were revolutionary, using these new techniques. We had very accomplished studio engineers and producers, but they had never tried to do what we were doing.

No one knew how to do it. A great deal of the disc we were just figuring out a process that worked for us...

And what process was that?

We'd choose the song, we'd decide what kind of sound we wanted this to be: lots of double tracking or very simple? First we'd lay down a click track, just to keep the rhythm, then we'd have a keyboard track to keep us in key playing in our headphones. The lead singer, whichever of us it was, would go in and do what you call a dummy lead, something to give everyone a reference. Then, all the back up parts, either together around one mike or four separate mikes, depending on what kind of sound we wanted, thickly blended sound (that's what we'd do with one mike) or separation, a stereo spread. It was trial and error; we were making up rules as we went.

Arnold would go in, do his bass part after the meat of the song was down there. While we're making backups that gives lead and bass a chance to hear how the song is progressing, so by the time Arnold gets in there he's got a really good idea of where it's going. Now the lead singer has had a chance, he's had a couple of weeks to live with how the song's developing, then he redoes the whole song, his whole part.

Some songs seemed to take forever, some songs that we thought would be simple would be the hardest to lay down.

We were doing the Parachute Club's Rise Up, a great song, we said we can do a great job with it, but nobody could decide who was going to do lead. It was war for the lead!

The producer, everybody wanted the lead done differently and we all wanted to lead!

Big thick production numbers like "Stars Are Ours," that took a lot of time; it was almost a symphonic work. That took a long time because...

Well, I'm not really the best person to ask about production, studio work. I love getting up in front of audiences, but in the studio I suffer from red-light-itis. I can sing very happily when I don't think anybody's around but as soon as somebody says "Okay, let's record this now," my voice goes, "uugh. No one's listening to this." Some people love the studio, making a perfect version of this song. But I don't like having those guys behind the glass, I go "No, no this is unreal, they've heard [the song] now how many times?"

What was original about One Size Fits All *is that you had someone doing drum tracks. How'd that come about?*

Steve Negus, he was in Saga, which was a big Canadian band back then and we were looking for someone, we were experimenting with adding some rhythm. Again we were recording at Sounds Interchange when he was in another studio doing some drum work for Saga. At that time there was a buzz in the city about us, and constantly people were coming into our recording session. It was very exciting; we were really complimented that established musicians were finding us, were interested...it wasn't really distracting it was encouraging. We knew of his work so we asked him to participate.

You switched gears after a couple of years from being a dinner theatre sort of act to a touring group.

We started off as a cabaret act, our first big gig in Basin Street jazz club we sold the place out for weeks and weeks and weeks. Coming from our musical theatre background, we made it into an act; we had scripted, dramatic pieces between songs. When we went to the concert stage, that was when there was a slight change in our act. We reinforced a strictly musical experience. We aimed more towards a stage act.

A lot of the promoters wouldn't back us when we wanted to go to the concert stage. They said, "You're a cabaret act." So what did we do? Just like with the record, we did it ourselves. We independently rented the main concert hall in Toronto, Massey Hall. We sold it. We got rave reviews. It was our first legitimate concert show and after that of course we said, "We'll choose which [concert promoter] we want to go with." From the very beginning we were four guys and no band and everybody said, "I don't think so; it's not gonna happen." But we said we're gonna plunge in and so we did it ourselves.

We were getting such incredible responses from the audiences. Even though the business people—the suits— didn't understand, just from the feedback from the audiences we knew we were doing the right thing.

What do you consider highlights of the years you and Marc were in The Nylons?

Our first Massey Hall show was definitely a landmark in the decade I was with the band. There were some moments I remember were big—Carnegie Hall, touring Europe, playing the Royal Albert Hall, doing the Tonight Show...

The first place we went to start making our fan base national was out in Vancouver. We were just adopted by the city. The fans in Vancouver were amazing. It was another shot in the arm: "This isn't a local phenomenon, they'll like us in other cities!" Vancouver crowds were some of the best—we played a place in Stanley Park called the Malkin Bowl, an outdoor ampitheatre—this is interesting—no music groups were allowed there, the city guys thought it would make the crowd too rowdy. No music groups, but they did let local theatre in there in the summer so the director of the theatre company brought us in as part of his summer theatre program! Malkin Bowl was just packed, standing room only, thousands of people, we got rave reviews. So the city had to acknowledge that we were there. From then on, they didn't take away the ban on music groups, but they made us the exception. We were the only music group to play there.

There's one song I just saw The Nylons do again in concert that I know you performed at the very beginning—Bruce Springsteen's "Fire," with that great moment at the end where The Nylons all brandish lit cigarette lighters. Why did that never get on an album?

I don't know why we never recorded "Fire." Every time we were working on an album, I'd say, "Let's do 'Fire.'" But no. I think it was too simple.

That period was where we were greatly influenced by Peter Mann, for better or worse. Lots of our stuff was too basic for Peter Mann; it had to be big, it had to be lavish for Peter. That was one of my problems, working with him later on we'd just say, "Hey, we'll do a very simple version of something," and he'd not like it. "We're doing this very simple, Peter, not with giant choirs!"

"Dream" was one of the very first songs we learned. There's so many things that are exactly the same since the first time we performed. Like "Fire" at the ending. We had no special effects; we said, "let's get Bic lighters," and it still works!

Arnold does "Silhouettes" the way we've always done it, he does a bit that originated with Ralph Cole. Ralph Cole developed the talking session, that very bit. When Arnold joined, we said, "Arnold, do it like this, this works: you have to go down and bug a girl in the front row in the middle of the song, and it has to end 'Don't I buy you new Nylons every week?'"

36

So much was just us having fun, we just came up with off the top of our heads, and it's still working after all these years.

The pattern of the first five albums seems to be: one song for Claude, two songs for Arnold, the rest group songs or split between you and Marc. Was that on purpose?

It was not a conscious thing, at least not at the beginning. Claude's voice is a unique voice, it's very, very high. It's not as easy to find a song for him that works in that range. Claude also was never a really trained singer. It may be he was not as confident in his ability to sing lead instead of just backup. That's just what I'm thinking.

When we started working with producers—even though we co-produced everything—they'd say, "Paul has a very commercial sounding voice, like white rock and roll." I'd never thought I would sing the lead on "Kiss Him Goodbye." I just said, "I know it would be a good crowd pleaser" and then they said, "Paul should sing this." I happened to think Arnold had one of the greatest lead voices anywhere. I just loved to hear the sound of his voice. So "Chain Gang" was my suggestion, I just knew he'd do a great job with it. We were always giving everybody a chance in the spotlight. No one person made or broke the group. Our strength was the four of us. It made the whole thing stronger. Claude and Arnold had a lot of interplay in the actual show, the bass is always kind of in your face. They've already got places of distinction, but we showcased those voices too. It was really just...it evolved.

Why is there a different running order and different songs on different albums?

That was the decision of different record companies, especially in the states. They said, "Well, geeze, could you take this song off and put this one on?" I remember one of my songs was totally cut. Who knows why. That was a business decision made by these suits, y'know? We kept strong artistic control throughout the whole process, but you don't want to alienate your record company, so if we didn't think it really mattered, we went with their decision.

Why did you quit the group?

I had just been doing it too long. I was totally nuts. Our career was peaking, but I was going nuts. It was real Michael Jordan syndrome. [Author's note: at the time of this interview, Michael Jordan had just announced his retirement.] When I heard Michael Jordan, I knew what he was going through, I thought, "I know exactly what you're talking about, I've been there." Though they think you're crazy, you know? I desperately needed a break. It was just a lot of hard, intensive work. Working like we were, there's no such thing as a relationship. I had been on the road for ten years. And yes, I admit there were some artistic differences. I had different ideas about what we were shooting at, where the group should be going.

I had no right to insist everybody do it my way.

What was "your way"?

I wanted to get to a more simplified sound. By the time I left I just thought the arrangements had gotten too overblown. I had started to kind of miss the naked, vulnerable quality. I was also strictly proud of this—trying to make a cappella a commercial success. My ambition from the very beginning was to get this music out to the masses. A lot of my suggestions for songs reflected that. When I suggested Kiss Him Goodbye, everybody said, "Are you kidding?" And I said, "Look, I know it's totally mindless. I'm not saying this is my favorite song, I'm saying we will get a top ten hit in the states." And it worked. That was another thing I was always going for in choosing the songs— it had to have some major artistic merit or it had to be a hit— nothing in the middle. We don't need filler here.

I always said just by doing this a cappella stuff, that's just enough, it's an artistic statement in itself. We were unique, revolutionary even. That was good enough. Our instinct on where to take it was already on the mark.

Peter Mann was into the music and it didn't matter to him whether or not it was going to be a hit. He was dragging his feet all the way on that one [Kiss Him Goodbye]. Peter Mann didn't want to have a part of that. So we said, "You don't have to work on the song then. We'll find another producer." And we did! There was a turning point for the band. I put my foot down and said, "Look, we've got to go for this. Let's go for the commercial hit record." It worked, it was on Billboard...

[No other a cappella group] can say that. We are still the most played a cappella group in the world. I thought, "Great! The guys will see all this success, they will get where I'm coming from. Right after that record, there was a meeting where it was said "Well! We won't do another album like that!" I thought, "We just got our most successful album, and you don't want to do that again? Uh oh. It might be time to think about something different." We had found our groove, we were happening, and we wanted to go back to Peter Mann and a less commercial album? When that happened I just said, "Aw...maybe it's time to rethink being here." We were just going in different directions.

Tell me about how you got along with Marc.

I've had people describe [my relationship with Marc] as oil and water. It was the classic Lennon and McCartney. We weren't the closest of friends but we brought out the best in each other. I had a huge amount of respect for his voice. I think that there was a bit of frustration for Marc—Marc worked very hard on keeping his voice in great shape, taking vocal coaching all the way through. He worked hard writing songs. All this stuff came easy for me. I didn't think about it. "You need somebody to sing? I'll sing. You need songs? I'll write songs."

I'd smoke cigarettes. Marc probably thought, "Why do I have to work so hard, goddamit it?"

We were so close, you're closer than in any other band [where] you each have your own little world. That's not the same kind of closeness as singing harmony. There's such incredible scrutiny. It's hard to be that close for that long so the stress was high.

When did you learn Marc was HIV positive?

I'm not sure of the exact year. Two years before the last album, so right during or just before we put out Happy Together. Now that's back a long time ago when there was more of a stigma attached to it. I know Marc did not want anyone to know. And though, you know, we weren't the closest of friends, he told me before telling all the other guys.

You have to put it in the context of the time. We respected his decision not to tell anyone. The hard part was everybody always thought Marc was a bit of a hypochondriac, he'd come in saying, "I'm not so sure I could sing this song tonight..." We were just used to his little ailments where he'd be thinking he's sick all day and can't sing and then he'd get out on stage and have a triumphant show. We just thought it was some more of that.

Only after the Rockapella album did [his health] start really going downhill.

Claude Morrison

A founding member of The Nylons; his falsetto is a trademark of the group

Let's set the scene. What was Toronto like in the mid-'70s?

I guess Toronto was culturally at something of a crossroads. The CN Tower, a major communications tower, which is something of a symbol of Toronto, was an indication of the diversity, there was a lot of multiculturalism going on, a lot of access to American media, because of our proximity to the border. We [the members of The Nylons] sprung up out of the theatre community. That was what we all were, out of work, or between jobs, singers, actors, and dancers. Toronto has a very vibrant, theatre community—actually, it's the third largest English speaking theatre centre after New York and London—even at that time, certainly even more so now.

[Marc] was doing some work at the Stratford Festival, which is a couple hours' west of here. People will joke around that Torontonians claim their city to be the centre of the universe. I guess if you wanted in on the action, Toronto was the place to come. Even if you ended up doing regional theatre, a great many times a production would be cast out of Toronto. So I think that's probably the lure that brought him to Toronto.

A high school friend said Marc was intimidated by Toronto at first.

He was born in Ottawa and spent his early teens in Ottawa and before that was living just outside of Halifax because his father was in the navy, so they moved around a bit. He also went to school in Edmonton, none of which are cities as big as Toronto, so maybe he just felt a little bit intimidated by the size of the big city. Y'know it's like the

41

equivalent of somebody going to New York. Whenever I go to New York I think, boy, it's exciting to come to New York, but I don't think I'd want to live there. Just too much going on. I think, "You people really need to chill out."

How did you meet Marc?

I knew Marc because he and Ian were living in the same house as a guy that I knew, Mark Russell, whom I was doing a show with, in the summer of '78. It was a production of Oklahoma, and Paul Cooper also was in that production. Mark Russell was a roommate with Ian Wallace, so Marc Connors was around a lot. And later on, when I did a production of "Kiss Me Kate," right around this time, '78, Marc Connors and Paul Cooper and a couple others came to see the show—it was in London, Ontario, about two hours west of here. And little did I know that they were sussing me out. They were already talking about starting this group, that it was going to be a cappella, and Marc had taken note of the fact that I had this falsetto. So they actually came down to London and saw the show.

Paul said the day they went to see "Kiss Me Kate," the power had gone out in the theatre, so the whole cast sat around backstage singing songs to a guitar.

That's right. And I had the guitar. I forgot about that— that's right! That sort of makes it like fate, because again, they came backstage, and I was playing the guitar, and everybody was singing in the dark here, illuminated only by candles. That was a further step in this audition that I didn't know was taking place. They took note of the fact that I had some technical knowledge of music, which came in handy.

Paul's right, that did happen that way. And I remember they couldn't stick around after the show, but I remember Paul leaving me a note saying "Claude, great show, gotta run, gotta get back to TO". But I was pleased they had driven all that way to see the show.

42

Later on I ended up in the hospital with the recurrence of an intestinal condition and Marc came to visit me in the hospital. He said, "Hurry up and get well because this group is really going to start and we're going to go all over the world and we're going to record and be famous, and we want you in it." And I said, "Oh, OK, well, that's…"—I was a bit skeptical, but I thought, what the hell, I'm recuperating, there's nothing better to do, so why not? So I got out of the hospital, and we rehearsed. Those guys had been rehearsing and I just sort of plugged into the arrangements, and two days later we made our debut at Scoops, which was this eatery in a fashionable part of Toronto. Monday nights they had a "sing for your supper" kind of thing. So we sang four songs and I think we had to repeat one of them because people just wouldn't stop. It was a small crowd, a small sleepy crowd, didn't know what to expect, and it was sort of the equivalent of blowing the roof off—as much as a small, sleepy crowd can blow the roof off. As I recall, we had no encores prepared, so we had to do one of the numbers over again.

What songs did you do?

I don't know which one we did a second time, but I do know the four—I even remember the order. 'Cause even then we were putting together a show. We wanted a beginning, a middle, and a closing. Being from theatre, we thought in those terms. The opener was "You Got Me Running, You Got Me Hiding" which we sort of stole off of a Persuasions album; [the second was] "What a Piece of Work Is Man," which is by Shakespeare, and set to music, and it's from the musical "Hair"—Denis [Simpson] had done "Hair," and Denis was our bass guy at the time; and the third was "Met Him On A Sunday," which we stole from Patti Labelle, from Laura Nyro's album "Gonna Take a Miracle" which had Patti Labelle singing on it; and the fourth was "Fire", Bruce Springsteen's "Fire," 'cause the Pointer Sisters had just had a big hit off it.

So it was kind of neat, 'cause "Fire" was at the time a very current hit, it wasn't like one of the oldies—all the others were more in the vein of oldies. But it was a pretty eclectic mix there actually, especially the Shakespeare one in the beginning. And prior to all this, I used to get together with Denis Simpson, before I even knew Marc or Paul, and sing with him, and ["What a Piece of Work Is Man"] was one of the numbers he and I used to sing together. So when Marc visited me in the hospital and said, "Hurry up. Come on. Get well," I knew that Denis was part of the group. And I thought, "Well that's great, 'cause I know Denis, he's great to work with, he's got a really incredible energy, and that'll be a lot of fun." And we both knew the song. It was a matter of the other two guys plugging into it. And being from the theatre, they knew the song too, 'cause theatre people know musicals.

Had you worked up any choreography?

It was all we could do to remember our parts and not bump into the furniture. It was on a tiny little stage and it was just the four of us. So, no, we just went from song to song, it wasn't so advanced that we had a whole lot of rehearsed patter in between it or anything. The performance on the whole probably didn't take much more than ten or fifteen minutes.

Not long after that, based on how much we enjoyed it and it seemed like the response was good, we just sort of resolved to play any place where people could listen to us. Fashion shows, benefits, parties, you name it. There was one party at this house Paul was living in on Spadina Avenue across from the El Macombo which is a famous old rock'n'roll club. We sang at that, and among the guests there was this guy I knew who had given me my first Equity job about a year previous to this named Taras Shipowick. I had run into him and said, "Why not come to this party? Just check out what we're doing. We're singing in this group." He knew who Marc was, and Denis, and Paul.

44

So he came to the party, and then after, he approached us and said, "Well, I had a reason for wanting to check this out. I've been put in charge of this nightclub that's gonna be opening up and we need entertainment." So he said "I'll front you a pre-production budget of $2000, and you get some costumes happening, and expand your repertoire, so you can make an evening out of it." So we did. I thought, my gosh, is this going to hold somebody's interest over the course of a whole evening? But we did, and we opened on the 16th of May, of 1979, and it was originally supposed to go for two weeks, and it ended up being held over for another four.

[Shipowick] was a director and producer. I had met him, as I said, doing a production of "Joseph and the Amazing Technicolor Dreamcoat." He was choreographing the show. It was the first Equity production I ever did. In that sense, he's given me my first job twice.

[Our choreography] wasn't terribly complicated, because it wasn't really a whole lot of space. It wasn't a large stage. Everyone could dance or move, but some more so than others. And besides, when you're singing a cappella and you've only got two feet, pretty much it's left, right, left, right, left, right, variations on that. It wasn't the Swan Lake repertoire or anything like that. It started to develop and get a little more ambitious. Even if it wasn't choreographed as such, we lit it and we gave it a conceptual approach. Stephen Sondheim said that every song should be like a one-act play. It should develop, it should have a beginning, a middle, have an ending. So we approached it that way. The lights and the costumes and the choreography were all intertwined as would be expected from four people who had, as their roots, theatre training.

[Marc had done] experimental theatre, dancing, clowning, he'd done a lot of clowning. Ian Wallace as well. So—Marc was really a person of the theatre and had lots of really sort of outrageous concepts. He was quite fertile that way, he had a rich imagination and could come up with some

45

terrific concepts and ideas. Marc and Paul were both that way. They were very good idea people.

Let's talk a little about your material. What do you remember about doing Lion Sleeps Tonight?

Marc originally thought of Lion Sleeps Tonight as a lead for me to do. And then when we got the single, and we heard this descant, that goes even higher than the lead vocal does, it got turned around, so Marc ended up doing the lead, and I did this descant that goes over it all.

We didn't really consciously realize it [had a descant] until we sat down and listened to the Tokens' version of it. "Wait a minute? What's that?" That's how that got reworked.

Who decided to stage the song as though you were sitting round a campfire?

I'm not sure who it was—it's set in a jungle, so it was kind of a tribal, rootsy thing, a tribe gathering around the campfire, which is archetypal, it's classical, people need fire for warmth, to prepare food, for shelter, for illumination, for protection. It had a very universal, archetypal feel and approach to it.

We wanted to make it clear we were doing this out of respect for the material, not to spoof it or to send it up. Some ways we're having fun with some of it, but also to be respectful of it and bring something out of it that hadn't been explored that way.

The other do-it-yourself musical style at the time was punk rock. Did you feel any kinship with punk?

Philosophically I guess there was a kinship, in the sense of doing it ourselves and that we were treading new ground. Musically I don't think there was a whole lot in common. [Punk] was more angry, protest, a little bit violent. We didn't really see ourselves as that. But we were breaking new ground, had done something there wasn't any rules for. I remember one time Marc just saying, "I want my parents to be able to see this show and enjoy it. I don't want to come off as being rude or dirty or stupid or untalented." He was one for self-criticisms and he just maintained the standard. He was always the one saying, "C'mon, let's go over this again, let's do it again, we haven't got it right yet. Until we can sing it through from start to finish three times then we haven't got it right." So he was a real perfectionist and really demanding of himself, encouraging us all to adopt a high artistic standard.

Ralph [Cole, who was the bass after Denis] and I tended to be a bit more easygoing. I think we were just thrilled and pleased just getting good response. Paul and Marc I always considered to be the founders of the group. When people ask I say I'm a founding member, but I don't consider myself to have "founded" the group. That was Paul and Marc's original conception.

How did the personalities mesh?

Well, Paul and Marc definitely had their differences over the years. But I think that happens when two strong, creative forces get together. It's a difference in opinion, different approaches, different artistic styles. I think sometimes that kind of tension can be the thing that makes for great art. Lennon and McCartney both had very, very different styles of writing. Paul McCartney tended to be more lyrical, a little more, people would say, "florid" or flowery." Some people would even say "sappy." Whereas Lennon's approach was more hard-edged, a bit more cynical. So often, they would give each other's songs the thing that they needed. They would often write the bridge of each other's songs. I don't know if that specifically was the case with Paul and Marc, but I think their tensions resulted in some pretty interesting artistic ideas coming forth. Marc used to believe in the philosophy of Hegel's dialectic, taking

47

one idea and fusing it with another idea and out of that comes a third idea which has the best parts of both of them.

It sounds a bit like harmony—taking disparate elements and merging them together.

Harmony—the tension is created sometimes by notes rubbing together to create overtones. So sometimes you're hearing more than just four parts in that harmony. In the early days people used to cock their heads and say, "I swear I'm hearing five or six parts." At first we thought, "whooah. Spooky." And then we realized there is a sonic explanation for that—the vibrations caused when certain notes rub together create another note. So it makes for five- or six-part harmony, not just a four-part harmony, even though there's only four people standing there.

Had you considered singing professionally before joining The Nylons?

I'd always wanted to be a singer but it was something I thought, "Oh, that'll just be a dream." Before the group got started, I was working as a dancer, a dancer who could sing, who was open to acting, whatever—but I was just going to any audition that came along, for the opportunity of it. I wasn't casting about professionally for long before the group got started.

Marc, by comparison, started acting professionally in...?

...'71 or '72. He'd spent a couple of seasons at Stratford, a couple seasons at Charlottetown, which is a summer theatre festival in Prince Edward Island, on the east coast of Canada. He had done a lot of alternative theatre, clowning, experimental theatre, regional musicals. So he had a much broader resume than I did. So for me—Denis Simpson had done Broadway, and Marc and Paul both had these rather extensive bios, so I was definitely the baby of the group, in terms of age and in terms of experience. So back then I was just happy to be there. And feeling quite honoured to be among these four people who were obviously really, really talented and who saw fit to include me in their group.

I heard a rumour once Marc had sung backup on a Patti Labelle recording. Is that true?

Marc adored Patti Labelle, and if he had ever sung backup for Patti Labelle I'd know it. I know he was a big, big, big Patti Labelle fan. He thought the sun just rose and shone on Patti Labelle. He loved all the Motown stuff. Definitely he had a thing for Patti Labelle and the Bluebells. She was great.

What about Laura Nyro? I hear a lot of similarities between your version of "Up on the Roof" and hers, the one on her album Christmas and the Beads of Sweat.

We stole her version (laughs). And "Met Him on a Sunday" came from that Laura Nyro album, Gonna Take A Miracle, with Patti Labelle and the Bluebells on it. I think Paul had it. I had a copy of one, Paul had a copy of one. I think we all real admirers of Laura Nyro. She was a pretty pre-eminent songwriter during that period.

Whose idea was it to do "Up on the Roof"?

I think that was probably Marc. We stole two versions of it. We took that from Laura Nyro and from James Taylor had also recorded it not too long before that, and so, again, Hegel's dialectic, right? We took the best out of both of those and came up with ours.

Your debut album sounds pretty good for a group that had never spent much time in a recording studio.

From my point of view you can definitely hear it's a first album. Because we weren't experienced in the studio, we hadn't done much work in the studio. And so we were kind of guided by producers, and engineers, and people who had been there before. For myself I know it always brought out, recording always did, still does, bring out my worst insecurities, because you're just under such a microscope. You can just hear, you can hear a breath. You can hear the smallest breath. It's just very very intimidating.

At one point I remember we were recording the American version of Lion Sleeps Tonight with Val Garay in Los Angeles. I was behind the mike and Val said, "Something wrong, Claude?" And I said, "Well, I just get a little bit insecure, this really brings out the insecurities in me, I'm kind of tightening up." And he said, "It's a little late to be insecure, don't you think? This is your fourth album." I appreciated it because it was his way of saying "You've gotten this far, obviously you have business being here, you have a right to be here, you're good enough to be here, stop beating yourself up and just relax and do it." So that was quite helpful to me.

What sort of memories do you have of Marc outside of the work? Being on the road all the time, I guess you probably got tired of seeing each other...

To some extent that's true, but no, I hung out with both Marc and Paul a great deal—not at the same time usually. Marc and I were both brought up lily-white Canadians, Catholic, and so if you know anything about the Catholic Church, there's just a kind of a shared sense of humour that you have. I think we both sort of—there were many many times when I just knew what Marc was thinking, and I knew

50

that he knew what I was thinking. There were times when we'd just sort of look at each other, just in the middle of this or that, what's going on, we just had the same thought. Often I think it was because of our shared Catholic upbringing, just sort of gave us a similar sensibility there.

But I miss Marc—truly, I miss him every day. His fingerprints are all over what we do even today. It's just—after he died, [continuing with The Nylons] for me was one of the things that made it a lot easier because he truly lived on without sounding corny or overly sentimental or anything like that. I understand what people mean when they say when somebody lives on through something else. This is a real example of that. Because it is to a fair extent his legacy and so as a result I just think of him every day. That's not an exaggeration. And I wish he were still around. I often think: Gosh, what would he have done in this situation?

After Marc died, Billy Newton-Davis joined the group, and through Billy I met Victor, who is my partner, who I've been with for the last eight years.

And Victor has said a couple of times, "You know, it's so strange, I've heard so much about Marc, I've lived with so much of what he's done, but I never met him. I never even saw him in performance."

Then he said, "Yet I feel like I know him because I've lived with so much of what he's done." The fact that Marc and I were close, that Marc was such a big part of my life. And he said, "In an indirect way, I never would have met you if it weren't for Marc." So there's another reason why I think of Marc every day.

Micah Barnes

He replaced Paul Cooper in 1990; he and Marc can be heard together on Four on the Floor

How long were you a Nylons fan?

I came on kinda early (laughs). I mean, I was really a kid when they got going. I went to see them at...Basin Street Cabaret. Oh my god! Oh yeah, I was in the audience during the run. Isn't that the best? I couldn't believe how much I loved these four hometown musical comedy homos. I mean it was brilliant for me because up to that point we hadn't had anybody doing anything like that. And they were sassy and savvy and just sexy and silly—they were all the s words (laughs). And splendid. I just loved them. And of course they were my hometown heroes.

I remember—I was also performing at that point, I had a punk band and after that, like a jazz cabaret thing. I've got a crazy story for you. Honey, I auditioned for them when they were looking to replace Denis Simpson. They put a call out for a bass singer, which I was not, but I went anyway and I sang them my songs. Actually we all smoked a big joint, Paul handed me a joint (laughs) and we all did a craaaazy audition in which I sang for them at the piano in Paul's apartment on Yonge Street and they sang a couple of songs for me, a couple of which ended up on One Size Fits All. Time and perhaps the joint erases what they were but I remember when the record came out I was like "Oh my God, I heard that!" (Laughs) I gotta tell ya it was so exciting hanging out with them. But I looked at them and said, "So I know I'm not a bass singer." And they knew I wasn't either.

I was one of the gay kids who was in the theatre and was completely inspired by their work and would continue to see them locally and always felt like "Wow! We have our own camp classic boy a cappella group!" You have to understand the city and the country was in their thrrralll, they were the

52

show business story. Hit records bring you a different kind of an audience, they didn't wanna just play the downtown cabaret of every city, they wanted to play concerts—and they did. They made great, great strides (considering the day) of trying to create a whole theatrical presentation much inspired by certainly the work of Bette Midler, who was taking essentially a cabaret art form into the rock concert venue.

It would have made sense for [Midler] in the early days to have just fired the Harlettes and hired The Nylons. They were campy enough, they were fun enough, and they sure were sassy. That that didn't happen was probably a career moment. You either stay cabaret, or campy, or a gay secret, or you get out there in the mainstream and start making your noise to everybody. They were able to do that. It's terrific that they were on every college campus playlist. They were alternative before alternative existed.

They came under a lot of fire from purists, but they were never trying to be purists, they were all about trying to use the machinery—The Nylons were about usin' what ya got to put on a show!

They played during the Toronto Film Festival one year. At the time [it] was not yet the big deal it became, but it was very exciting for us locals in that we would all get to see brilliant international film. Bette Midler was opening "Divine Madness" one of the evenings, and The Nylons were going to sing for her at the afterparty. And the mikes broke and the system broke, and they sang without mikes; no one could hear them, and they were really upset. They were leaving the party as I bumped into Marc in the hall and he said, "It didn't go great because the system broke down, but Bette was really cool about it and she understood; and she seemed to like it anyway." And I remember thinking, "Wow, like these are my professional pals." Hee hee! Little did I know, little did I know.

And I took my father and my youngest brother to see them at the Bathurst Street theatre, one of their first concert tours with full production and costumes and big sets, and

[we] were blown a-way. Loved it, loved it, loved it. They were my hometown heroes.

Did you love the albums as much as their concerts?

NO. I did not. I was not a fan of the records as much as I was of the live shows. I didn't feel that they had translated—probably One Size Fits All was the best one. But the rest of the records I wasn't as happy about. And when I was asked to join the group, when it was really on the table, I turned to my at the time boyfriend Rene Highway and said, "Y'know I really don't love the records, but I love the live show." And he looked at me and he said, "Well, now you have an opportunity to make the records better." And I thought, "Well, that's quite a way of saying it."

Most Nylons fans would think this is sacrilegious but they would also agree that it's a better live show. It's a difficult act to capture on record because they were live performers first and foremost and singers sometimes second. But everybody improved as a singer as they went on. I mean, in the early days [at] Basin St. Cabaret it did not yet have the musical intelligence that Peter Mann would bring to the group and that the group would develop on its own. It was rough, but it was kinetic; and it was so smart and so much fun that it didn't matter all the harmonies weren't there yet.

Tell me what you remember about Marc.

Marc was my mentor. I knew that he was ill when I was auditioning for the group. Part of why I joined was because I recognized a teacher for me in Marc Connors and I knew that I would have a limited amount of time to work with him because he was ill. So that was one of the great motivators for me. He knew it too. He took on the role and the responsibilities of a mentor. In discussing with me whether it was a good idea for me to join the group, he said, "Perhaps this will complete the knowledge you need to create music in

54

your own career, or create a more fulfilling career on your own later" and of course he proved to be correct.

Under Marc's tutelage I learned a 150 percent commitment to the task at hand, a direct correlation between the hard work of rehearsal and the seeming ease in concert performance. He taught me that an artist that continues to grow technically and an artist who's continually seeking to grow is in fact the artist that is able to give back to the audience in the most complete way and their careers tend to be healthier.

And he taught me how to handle my business (speaks in a clipped, almost British style) "in a forthright and direct manner" and to ask questions where needed and to not let business matters simply go by the wayside—because after all we artists don't like to deal with that. He helped me put the reins of control in my own hands both of the Nylons career and of my own career. When he passed I sat at the table very much in the place that he had sat, questioning and poking and trying to find the larger picture and to inspire the group, to make us as good as we possibly could be.

Marc gave me a love for who I am and an acceptance of who I am, an understanding of who I am. It went both ways. There was a period where we were almost crushed out on each other even though we weren't ever lovers. There was this sense of being delighted in each other and what we both were sharing. We were also, in a subtle way, in competition in that we were both leads, the co-leads at the time.

How I came to be in the group has a lot to do with Marc Connors' decision that I really was the right guy for the job, his ability to communicate that to me, and for me to respond to his intelligence and his clarity as an artist and as a person. He's one of the most intelligent people I've ever known in my life, and most dedicated to seeing his creations through. And I really changed as a person because of coming into contact with him. That's why I'm delighted to be telling you about Marc and my experience with him but also I'm just amazed that I came into contact with him on such a close level, that I toured with him and we were with each other every day in rehearsal or in performance. I got the motherlode from him.

Your companion Rene Highway and Marc's companion Ian Wallace did productions together, didn't they?

Yeah, most specifically "Beavers" and a couple other [works]. Native Earth, the company Rene was closely associated with, did a lot of coproductions and cowork with a company Ian was with, the Theatre Resource Centre. So the fact that Marc's man was a performance artist/clown and my man was a dancer/director and that Ian's mentor Pochinko took a lot of his stuff from Native American work and Rene was native—there was a whole realm of understanding.

Marc was an extremely spiritual person and his connection to spirit was extremely strong. We bonded very deeply over A Course in Miracles which was a book we were both working out of when we met. He just turned to me one day on tour, we were in Banff, and he said, "Honey, there's a book I'm working out of I would love to lend to you" and I said, "Really? What is it?" I knew exactly what it was, and he said, "A Course in Miracles" and I opened the door to my hotel room and of course there was my copy right on the bed.

I'd been working out of it in preparation for the fact that I would lose so many of my loved ones. And Marc knew that I would be his voice in the group after he passed and he gave me a lot of strength for that and I felt that I had a role to play after his death. It wasn't always a popular role with the others. I don't regret having sort of slid into his shoes for a period of time but it wasn't my group to run. I knew that. So it was smart for me to step back. I had to go on and do my own work. Marc always understood that I would do that.

Let's talk a little about the rapport between Marc and The Nylons' arranger, Peter Mann.

Peter and Marc worked very instinctively together. They really thought along the same lines about harmony and music and getting that perfect ring. They were a wonderful team and I was very happy to sort of try to fit myself into that vibe, although I know I brought a kind of a chaotic spirit to it.

Marc was so dedicated to creating beauty in the world and so disciplined about his art that he was able to overcome the physical distractions and truly burn in the brightest of manners. As he got sicker on stage his voice became more bell-like, more beautiful; he became more pure essence of himself. He'd always been ruggedly beautiful in an almost too pretty, Prince Charming kind of way. As his looks shifted and he felt his looks were going he gave in a more pure, spiritual kind of way to the act of performing. It was less of the sassy, less of the gay, a little bit less of the showboy and a lot more of the evolved spiritual man which he truly was.

And I think he replaced that kind of burning ego which most great artists have—and Marc was a great artist and he did have it—but I could see him letting go of it. A Course in Miracles was a big part of that, [he was] beginning to really just shine with love. He let go of his ego—you have to. I mean you have to if you're going to learn your lessons as a human being on this planet and he truly completed his lessons, I think, by the time he was leaving us.

You know, of course, this is going to be about Marc more than it is about The Nylons, though perhaps someday someone will write a book about The Nylons.

I hope someone will do The Nylons' story. It's really worth telling. It doesn't matter what angle they go for; Paul

57

and Claude will have really different attitudes about exactly the same thing and so Marc would have. Marc and Paul were extremely agitated with each other a lot of the time and I was partly brought in because they just needed to be able to move forward as a group. They couldn't rehearse.

So I mean I think there was a huge burst of energy when I first joined. Unfortunately that record [Four on the Floor] was made at the end of Marc's life, and right after Rene had passed, so we were kinda working on a deficit—I had just lost my lover and I couldn't even talk. If you ask the guys about me during that period they'll all say that I was like a very gloomy catatonic presence. I was suicidal. I actually quietly was screaming, my sleeping pills ran out and I was trapped…it was just horrible, horrible for me, I'm amazed I was able to do those concerts—but I dunno…(sighs) I mean I didn't make the other records. I don't know what the spirit of them were, but I know that they spent a long, looong time arguing, mad at each other because someone's favorite song didn't get on, a lot of fighting in that group.

It's what harmony's about, though, isn't it? Trying to bring something beautiful out of different elements.

Yes. That's true. I thought it did. I think Paul and Marc were actually perfect for each other. They were in competition, so it created an atmosphere that was charged and forced them both to be the best they could be. There are a lot of arguments for why a group has a perfect flavour or a perfect mixture of ingredients and that was a pretty perfect mix. You know, had Marc lived I think he and I would have proved to be a pretty damn good mix, for a while anyway.

I loved, *loved* performing with Marc and I loved being with him. Even when we had disagreements, which we did have, I was insecure about my place in the group, I mean I was a good ten years younger than people in the group. [I had] this sense for me that I was of another generation and that I was punk rock, new wave, hip hop.

I loved Marc, I mean I really did; but he was a bag of trouble too. He could be—he was very, very witty and very much the banterer in a very wicked manner. When he wanted to hit you between the eyes it was a direct hit. Cause he was extremely intelligent and competitive and very fierce. He was a fierce, ruling diva. Truly. As a gay man I know that survival skill is all we have sometimes. He was a powerhouse. Remember his father was in the military. He comes from the kind of family where masculinity or power, a certain brand of masculinity was seen as okay. He was always gonna be the faggot son but he created such a fierce power in the world anyway.

You have been more politically active as a gay man and as an entertainer than Marc was. What's your take on that?

The Nylons, the core members of the group, were of a generation that would not see themselves as needing to use their lives or use their work in a political way. It was daring enough that there was tongue-in-cheek playfulness between men on stage. All power to a bunch of guys who didn't let their sexuality—not all the members were gay—stop them from communicating in the world. Because I'm of a different generation, I myself had a lot of difficulty with going back in the closet in order to be a member of The Nylons. I certainly had my knuckles rapped, and rightly so, for acting as the renegade and giving interviews to the press in which I was openly gay and speaking about political issues of the day, which for me were extremely personal. My generation being the "ACT-UP" generation, it was a very strange thing to be caught in the dichotomy.

Here's a great example. We were booked to play San Francisco during the March on Washington. It was a historic march, and all of San Francisco was in Washington. And here were The Nylons, outmoded dinosaurs if ever there were any, playing to an audience of older gay men who weren't politicized enough to be in Washington. That meant that we were no longer on the important front page of gay culture. That was difficult for me, as a person, but also, I think, for the group—to start to have to contend with health issues right at a time when they could have been a leader [with] Melissa Etheridge and k.d. lang, been important spokespeople in Canada for a way of life that was under attack, for a sexuality which people were suddenly able to talk about openly. I don't fault the guys for being exactly who they are and for the generation that they're in. That's just the way things are. I'm a little older now, and I can accept that.

What was it like, dealing with Marc having AIDS?

I think the health issues were on everybody's mind the most. We were really worried for Marc. And we were worried that he was pushing himself. Everybody in the group in their own way tried to do our best to dissuade him from overusing his energy but he was not one to be dissuaded. He was a powerhouse that way. There was a huge cost to his body by maintaining [his energy level], but you know, I think he had the philosophy, "Look, if I'm going to go out, I'm going to go out singing."

When we met Lady Di for the [AIDS] Quilt—she was an honorary patron as were we of the Quilt and so we met in Toronto when the Princess was there—it was just after Marc died, about six months after Marc died. We were instructed not to make the Princess cry, because of course, we don't want too many photographs of her bawling in front of the press, right? Which of course I'd be horrified to admit that I was the bad boy that wanted to see her cry, certainly I did not.

She asked about Marc; she had certainly been prepped, and knew that we had lost a member to AIDS just recently. She asked about him and I told her what I'll tell you now, which is that he never sang so beautifully as when he was facing the end of his life. That it was incredible to stand beside him and to be witness to the way in which he used his body to make beautiful music just as he was having to let it go. And of course she began to cry and said, "There's so much work to be done" and of course melted all of us. We were just blown away. I was particularly pleased to have been able to give my Marc report to Princess Di. It made me feel like I was able to honor something of Marc's legend by having reported it to Lady Di. And of course with her death I just felt, goodness, that was really something, to lose her then.

I guess that's the story I was meshed in as Marc began to fall like a soldier, like when your sergeant falls or your captain falls, you don't know what you're going to do. You're still at war, you're still on the front lines, you have your instructions. It was important to me to see what I felt to be his vision through.

What sense do you have of the inspirations Marc had in music?

[Marc] absolutely loved early Dionne Warwick for the purity, for the inventiveness of the songs, and for the intelligent pop that she made with Bacharach. If you listen to his own writing, [you can tell it] really influenced him. He made tapes for me of her early stuff, he really wanted me to know. He loved the smarts of the American pop songwriters that delivered people-pleasing, emotional, three-minute mini-dramas. And he understood pop songwriting on a gut level. Although he was delighted by a lot of different kinds of music, he particularly embraced world music and he didn't get trapped in a cultural historian's approach to pop music, he understood it on a visceral level. I think that's what made him such a strong writer.

He was a little in awe of me musically and he was a little shy about the old-fashionedness of his tastes with me. Remember, I came in as a rock'n'roll kid. I think he felt sort of fuddy-duddy and old-fashioned. Look, if a Sonic Youth video came on the TV and I ran over to the TV and turned it up, because I loved it and that was the music that was speaking to me, that wasn't necessarily gonna make Marc wanna say, "Well, I really really love Frank Sinatra's phrasing!" But he loved the great singers—he got to work with a lot of them. He certainly loved k.d. lang, as we all did, and was particularly enamored of the kinds of singers that carve out a distinct personality and are able to communicate using material that they have invested in deeply. He watched and listened very closely to music.

It [our musical generation gap] was a gap in the way we were brought up as well. I come from bohemian hippies, intellectual hippies. I came up through punk rock. I mean, there's a big difference between a Judy Garland fag and a Patti Smith fag. It's the only way I can describe it.

Can you see him having favourites among the songs he performed?

"Amazon" was a really important song for him, he was a dedicated activist when it came to the environment and to animal rights. In fact he went so far as to almost miss a plane in order to make sure the authorities had been told this animal we'd seen in captivity at a local circus or something was in bad shape. "Amazon" being an environmentalist plea was important to him. We worked very hard on it. Although I think he loved all of his babies, I think the songs that he wrote he was especially and extremely pleased by, remembering that Paul Cooper was sort of the writer and Marc felt maybe like he had to fight for his own recognition as a writer. And I believe because he was not musically schooled, or he'd probably been told that he didn't have as good an ear as he had eventually developed, he still felt he was lacking in this area. I think it was a real personal point of pride that he was able to turn in such incredible songs.

I thought he knew gorgeous melodies like nobody else. He recognized the beauty of melody and harmony more than anybody in the group.

It's really a pleasure being able to speak about Marc, I mean it's sort of like setting the record straight, cause I think people might have thought because I was the new kid and that I was brought in just at the end of his being with the group that we weren't connected or that I was somehow at odds with Marc musically or something. I learned so much working with him. I guess that's pretty clear, that he was a mentor of mine, in fact one of the most important mentors I'll ever have in my life.

Karen Webb

Long-time fan of The Nylons who helped ensure Marc had his name on an AIDS memorial in Toronto. This chapter is written from my perspective with quotes from Karen.

While I was in Toronto looking for interview subjects for this book, I was fortunate enough to meet Karen Webb. I visited her on a very cold, snowy night, in the middle of the worst snowstorm Toronto had suffered in decades.

We ate pizza and chatted awhile, "Four on the Floor" on her stereo serving as backdrop for our conversation. Then she brought out her box of memorabilia.

"The very first time I saw The Nylons, I went after school," Karen told me. "I was in high school and my brothers were interested in them. We went down super early and we were in the fifth row. My brothers said 'Wow! We've never even been in the fifth row before!' And after that show I was so hooked, I would go straight after school or skip—I remember getting a new job and saying, 'I need to have a certain day off.' And the reason was that The Nylons were going to be performing."

To get information on upcoming shows, she kept up a steady correspondence with Julie Brown at Headquarters, The Nylons' management company. Julie was the assistant to their manager, Wayne Thompson. Karen wrote so often, she says, "the very first time I met Wayne, he was able to recite my address." She went to countless shows, always hanging around afterwards to chat with the band. "It was so great. For years and years I'd go to Ontario Place and I'd hang around and hang around and finally Julie or somebody would recognize me and say 'Okay, she can come in' and I'd be pulling past the sea of people saying 'Wow, how'd you manage that?' But after a couple of years I'd actually <u>be</u> on the backstage list. I'd say 'Excuse me, Karen Webb' and they'd check the list.

"Everyone else'd say 'WOW! How'd you do that?' And I'd say 'Well, it's just perseverance, ten years of what you've been doing. You're doing a good job.' I'd say, 'The Nylons are great, most times they will come out and say hello, so just hang in there. Sorry guys, I gotta go in!'"

Karen pulled from her memorabilia box autographed pictures, glittering stockings that had decorated The Nylons' microphones in the early days, scrapbooks with notes on countless shows.

"'Nylons in concert, Stephen Leacock Theatre, Keswick,'" she read from a ticket stub. Then she explained, " This was the best place to see them because the theatre was so small the stage was literally where my television is. We were right there. It seemed very cozy and very small. We had also brought flowers that time."

Marc autographed one picture with "Remember me as I was. Marco Connors." "Good old Marco Lamour," Karen said. "The guys would go off and do a costume change and Marc would stay on to do one of his romance songs. It was great, and then he'd do 'Town Without Pity' and would rip open his shirt. That was the Marco Lamour song. Then he'd back off and the guys would come back on. It was pretty short but it was a popular bit—he was a popular figure."

Karen was proudest of the times when she was acknowledged by the guys from the stage. You can't go to concerts for years and not be noticed. Once she saw The Nylons at Massey Hall with a couple of friends. They all had front row seats and had brought along roses. At one point Arnold said, "I hate this song." Marc said, "Don't worry, Karen, he's only kidding." "Totally unexpected," Karen said, laughing. "When Marc sang 'Up on the Roof' I gave him a rose; he bent to kiss me and Arnold said 'Ladies and gentlemen—Marc and Karen!'"

At another show, when Marc was introducing 'Busy Tonight', Arnold was snickering in the background. "I laughed along and Marc said 'Shut up, Karen! I'd know that voice anywhere!' I have a very distinct laugh. They are very good with audience repartee, I see nothing wrong in yelling at them and making suggestions and all that."

She has fond memories of years of Nylons appearances at the Forum at Ontario Place, a popular lakeside theme park. She read me the description of one such concert in '87 or '88 from her journal: "Big line of families waiting to get in so I didn't get into the Forum until 10:10 am followed by a few other diehards"—("and this was for an 8:30 concert," she explained). "Soundchecks were around 4 o'clock. Marc was on first. They all came on for group check with four Ontario Place 'animals' (entertainers in animal costumes) and it was a mini-show. I think they were all having a lot of fun.

"Show was great. Lots of standing up and dancing. The audience was in the mood because we did The Wave and believe it or not an incredible 'O Canada'—the whole packed Forum stood and sang it. It was beautiful."

She echoed sentiments expressed by other fans. "They usually did Ontario Place twice a summer. It was a standard thing. When it stopped happening it was like, "What's going on here?" And now Ontario Place is no more. Now it's Molson Ampitheatre, got more of a mosh pit, meant for bigger shows."

Karen enjoyed talking with Claude, Paul, Arnold and Marc after the concerts. She waxed rhapsodic about unexpected privileges of long-term fandom, like the time when Marc asked her and her friends to look over some photos and tell him which were best suited for the cover of Rockapella. But in '88 she got up the nerve to include a lunch invitation in Christmas cards to Marc and to Arnold, her two favorite Nylons, and though Arnold never took up the invitation, Marc did. After a show in mid-June they set plans for the coming Wednesday (after a Tuesday radio interview), and Marc gave her his home phone number to confirm the arrangements. She read this story too from her journal:

"Lunch with Marc—June 13, 1989.

"After the show (Saturday, June 10th) I couldn't fall asleep—I was actually going to have lunch with Marc! We had left it that we would get together on Wednesday but I thought it out and really wanted to see the interview he was doing on Tuesday, which was the original plan. After many minutes of torture I called his number and left a message that if at all possible could we go back to Tuesday and please call me at work or home on Monday. He called at 10:20 pm— and for me I was still like in my early 20s, that was late— and told me where to be the next day. Arnold and [his wife] Chris were there. Unfortunately the interviewer had only the room for the two guys—he was telling me that I could come and listen to this radio interview but of course those radio interviewing rooms are very small so it wasn't possible.

"Marc and I went to a Japanese restaurant and we had about an hour and a half. It was a great time. I was honoured by what he was sharing with me. He also insisted on treating me which was not what I had planned." At this point she stopped reading and explained, "One of the things he asked me was how I'd feel if Paul left the group. This was very privileged information—'You're actually sharing this with me?' I couldn't believe it. So I gave him my personal insight on that. I didn't think the group would suffer. To me, although he's a fantastic performer, he was always so much more the showy guy.

Being a large person I know large people aren't considered you know, super-attractive and all that. In that sense, he's not taking away anything from the group, he's not giving anything to the group. I just said 'I can see he's got a good, basic voice and you need good, basic voices like that. But Claude would really be missed and Arnold would especially be missed—and, God, Marc, I'm here with you having lunch, you would definitely be missed! So of any of the four, I would say Paul would be the first one that I could see actually leaving the group.' So that's what I told him. But I just couldn't believe he was asking me what I thought, how it would affect the group.

It wasn't until September 14th of 1989 that the official announcement was made that Paul was leaving the group, but that led to Karen's discovery of other connections.

"I knew Micah [Barnes] in high school because I was in Grade 9 and he was in Grade 13. We were both in music and he was taking a theatre arts program in Grade 13. We got to know each other from all that. When he did his solo career his brother who was actually a year behind me was a drummer in his band. I went to see them several times. Then when I was keeping up with Julie and saying, 'Well, who's gonna be the next Nylon?' She said, 'Well, it's between two people, it's either So-and-so or Micah Barnes.' I said 'GET OUT!' So Micah said a couple of times after the show, 'Karen, it's always amazing. Whenever I see you, I think of high school, I think of my solo career, I think of the time now with The Nylons, it's like it's come full circle.'

"I thought he was really good with the group, I always felt Billy was not quite the right mix, there was something that didn't click. Arnold and Marc were always my top two if we're naming names."

The Nylons were often doing benefits, and at one of these they premiered a song called Amazon, a plea for the rain forests. Soon after, Karen gave Marc a certificate from the World Wildlife Fund that 4 acres of the Amazon had been saved in their honour. "Marc jumped up and gave me a big hug. Wayne said they should have [the certificate] framed to put up in the office. Claude said he wanted to develop on it."

We had spent about two hours sorting through memorabilia and paging through the journal when Karen said, "This was the bad news time." She read, "March the

25th, 1991. One of my friends called me around 6 p.m. and asked me when I'd finish work and when would I be home. I told her I'd be home by 9 and she said, "I'll be there." I thought it was a little unusual but since it was Oscar night I thought she just wanted to chat. She came with a couple of my other friends around 9:30. We laughed and watched the awards then at 9:45 she got very serious and told me to turn the TV off. She sat on the floor facing me and said, "Marc died this morning, Karen." Shock, and then the tears came. She'd called Wendy [at the office] out of the blue this morning and found out. She asked permission to tell us before it hit the papers. I really appreciated it. We talked until about 11:30 p.m. They left and I stayed up and watched the rest of the Oscars.

"Tuesday March 26th. Today it hit the papers. People at work could tell that I was upset about something. I had called Mom after I got up and told her. I started crying again and so I didn't really cry at work. I showed my boss the headline before the meeting so she understood. I never got so many phone calls before in a day, mostly the friends who'd been over the previous night. My brother even called to see if I knew. Julie called at 1 p.m., because she thought I'd called the office, and she told me about the visitation and the funeral. When I got home and saw it on CityTV, I cried again.

"Wednesday, March 27th. My friends and I walked to the Roscoe-Morrison Funeral Home. When we entered the building the first person we saw was Ian. He was coming down the stairs, smiling, and he hugged us all and showed us where to go. He told us to come to the front when we were ready. Everything was beautifully arranged, important things to Marc around his body, which was wrapped in white silk. Ian said, 'I didn't want to see him in a box.' Hugged Micah, Wendy from the office, Claude, Arnold and spent a large time hugging Julie. I cried a lot and as we left I spoke to Marc's mother. When I got home I called my boss and told her I wouldn't be in to work the next day—am too upset, and it means a lot to me to go to the funeral.

"Funeral 11:30 am. I was there by 10:45 am, met up with my friends at the coffeeshop. We sat in the middle of the funeral home's chapel. By the time the service started it was standing room only and they had a room set up with chairs and a TV screen so that others could see. Ian started the service—he hasn't cried yet. The girls say that it sounds like Marc talking. He sure has a strong inner strength.

A woman sang 'Up on the Roof' beautifully then a couple of Marc's friends spoke. Claude then sang Grown Man Cry with Arnold offering his help. That was amazing. [Claude] had also brought Marc a T-shirt back from Thailand with a dolphin and Ian said that he was going to send it with Marc. Claude also left a pitchpipe that he said all The Nylons had been given when the group first started and he was the only one who still had an original. Ian then said that Marc was going to share something and they played 'Up the Ladder to the Roof'.

During all the songs, Ian was mouthing the words, so were we all through our tears. Then Ian invited all of us to come up and say hello/goodbye to Marc. When we got there we noticed the long-stemmed rose that we had brought the night before was lying on the silk. That broke some of the girls and I was already crying.

We spoke to one of Marc's sisters. Hugged Arnold and Claude and as we were leaving we saw Chris, and when I hugged her I wasn't crying anymore. I felt I was giving her support. We saw Ian in the parking lot. The night before he had said "Remember his smile," and I had said, "Seeing your smile is giving me strength." This time I said "I am smiling now," and I was. I guess I was out of tears. I'm crying now and it's April 1st. Paul Cooper was in a van and we went over to say hello."

I asked her how much warning she had, if she even knew Marc was sick.

"I knew he was sick but it was denial. Because seeing him with the beard, I didn't like him with the beard, I even remember telling him that I didn't like the beard and then afterward feeling so ashamed like how dare I say such a thing and the last time I saw them backstage I hadn't been able to go over to talk to him or anything like that. You could tell he was not healthy. Little things piling up but you didn't want to accept it, you didn't want to think this could possibly be the case. He really performed up to the last minute. He was preparing to step down, but at the same time he wasn't there yet and he thought he could handle it and..." Her voice trailed off.

"I think we all sort of knew but since nobody was admitting to anything, then we let them go on with their cover story. But it was a shocker and I'm an easy person to cry anyway."

Marc Connors

These are pages from a journal he kept

November 23, 1990—on plane to San Francisco

Barry has asked me to do two exercises—one a sort of summation of my life—achievements and regrets. The other, a "what if" of my future, being as creative as possible. So...

I am dying. It's now clear I will not recover. I am sad for my parents and especially for Ian. And my sisters, friends and fans. My death will affect a wide circle of people. And yet I'm not really that important or significant. Altho [sic] who is? I guess I most wanted to be someone who contributed to people's lives, the way I cherish Chaplin or Tchaikovsky or so many book and filmmakers and actors. I've had some effect in that area—I've moved and excited people. I'm sorry I haven't left more of an intellectual legacy. Scripts, songs, ideas—especially wonderful stories. Maybe that's not my talent and yet if love were enough to make one talented I'd be one of the great storytellers. I love a story where all life's problems are surmounted by a sudden deeper understanding, a spiritual understanding, a renewed faith in the human spirit.

I am dying. I'm sorry not to have the chance to take my story further but I look back and see I've done much of what I wanted. As a child I was excitable, filled with fantasy and my own specialness, loving to perform for adults and earn their delight. I would swoon before visions of beauty—like the first time I heard Tchaikovsky on the Kistler's record player. I wanted to run away and live with the Indians when I was eleven and had read a history of the United States. It seemed to be a wonderful life—free, earthy, natural, exciting. My friend Kent and I made plywood war clubs for play. I wanted to sing like him but Mom said I wasn't the vocal lesson type and denied my request. I yearned for it but went underground until college. I fantasized in the bath and elsewhere that all was being recorded, someone was listening and noting as I sang my heart out or acted.

I loved the movies I snuck down to see every night after the family had gone to bed. I played the characters in the mirrors I spent more and more time gazing into. I knew I had greatness in me. I knew I couldn't feel this strongly and not be talented. Well, I acted. Sometimes it was great and I realized I had a unique talent—Godspell, Man of La Mancha, the Allen Gardens show, the excerpt from Big Bear, Cromwell in Man for All Seasons. I was a chameleon with great instincts. I discovered that I was a theatrical performer, not realistic. I wanted a mask.

I wanted to dance and in school and after I did. All those…concerts, all those classes, all the frustration with my posture, my knees and backaches, choreographing. At one point I wanted to be NIJINSKY, wore his t-shirt every day to class. I wanted to choreograph and dance the Rite of Spring. But I saw it wasn't my life. My greatest moment was Linda Rabin telling me I had "it" after a particularly hard and exciting class. I could have been great, she said. With that I had got what I needed and sort of ended my dance career with Marcus and Meira of which I am very proud. I've always felt I'd have something to contribute to choreography--a desire to make it more exciting and moving, strange, lovely, haunting.

I wanted to sing and I have, in spades. I've sung in ecstasy and misery, in good voice and almost none at all, with real artistry and poorly, onstage and on record. My major regret is that I wasn't more confident. I was always held back by my insecurities as a singer and actor especially. My hours of painful doubts and fears.

I-I-I-I! I've always been so self-obsessed. I hope that I have matured somewhat and have opened my eyes to others, opened my heart to their needs and lives. But for most of my life I was furiously pedaling the bike of Marc.

I wanted to direct someday, run an experimental theatre company. I saw them creating magic with almost no props or set. I felt I could create something beautiful and powerful. I always felt I had an instinct for how things should be, exciting, moving, powerful. But maybe the theatre's dead anyway and these are 19th century dreams. But I did direct Damn Yankees and that was one of the highs of my life and Marcus and Meira was wonderful. I put Starry Night together. I produced Ian's show. Nothing much caught the world's attention but I'm proud of them and happy with the fun I had doing them. To go onto the world stage—I don't know if I could have survived the stress anyway. I always wished I could be less nervous and anxious, not care if something succeeded. Have confidence and enjoyment and not worry. What a liberation that would have been. I left acting because I was so tied in knots that I couldn't enjoy myself, couldn't release my energies into the act, was constantly judging and commenting, always dissatisfied with the show, my performance, the director etc. I'm sorry my relationship with Cheryl collapsed altho it just had to and was no foundation for an artistic life. But we had an exciting and creative way of working that I cherish the memories of. Brave and idealistic.

I am proud I created the Nylons career but frustrated that we never ascended to the world fame and acceptance I'd hoped. And the monetary success I'd dreamed of. Maybe tho again I found a level of fame I was comfortable with, and financial level too. Some great artistic thrills (Please, Carnegie Hall, many shows, recording etc) and some of the worst days of my life. Surely the problems with Paul were sent as my great teacher.

I never thought I had any composing ability and to realize I did was one of the great moments in my life. To write Find the One I Love and A Million Ways was a revelation. I must mention Seth and how I used his ideas to program myself to be creative. He was one of the great spiritual enrichments of my life as is the Course of Miracles

74

as it continues to comfort and change me. I have never lost the need for spiritual consciousness. Thank God my mind rebelled from the Catholic Church and I went on my own search. I'm proud of my courage and vision.

Although denying I had much relationship to my intuitions, I actually was quite intuitive in my life. I sought out new phases in my career actively, blindly but with faith (usually). I'm sorry I was so scared, so anxious about survival, deep down worried about being "GOOD ENOUGH". I think it kept me bush league and never let my talents fly. So far, no farther. I loved biographies and devoured them especially in the latter years of my life. What was it they satisfied—a desire to be a pioneer, to be a player in the great times. A hunger for success? And yet a voice deep inside acknowledges that success is a chimera. I guess the person I need to impress is myself and there have been a few times I've done that...

I had two great loves in my life. They were great lessons. Dennis was a fantasy come true. My beautiful blonde Ukrainian lover. How I "fell in love" with him. I drank deep from that cup. And I gave myself with abandon. But there were bitter dregs at the bottom—he was insecure and fatally flawed, never accepting the one who loved him, always chasing after the "better" one. And it killed him. But I remember lying on a hillside under the moon and thanking God for being alive to love that much. I love you still Dennis and always will be grateful.

And Ian—the love of my life, the leprechaun, my guru, my lover, my friend, my keeper, my baby boy, my brother, my collaborator, my beautiful faun, my artist, my handyman, my nurse, my charge, my partner, my heartthrob, my conquest, my magic, my reason, my joy, my companion, my lifemate. I knew—my heart recognized him. He is the great miracle of my life—how different my life would have been without him. I learned so much from him—I learned how to

75

love without counting the cost, without trading, just giving. If I must leave him all I ask is that it not break his spirit which I fear is fragile when he is all alone. It would break my heart if this occurred.

We have always had such a lovely life together. The early years were full of fights and problems but when we settled down we always had a wonderful home and there was a grace to our lives, even the horrible infidelity of my affair with Normand was handled with grace. I'm sorry we didn't handle our sexual relationship with more wisdom. In other ways we drew apart and he retreated. His tendency to live an interior life, separate, was difficult for me to bear. It's changed a lot lately as this disease has made us understand our love and need for each other.

As I write all this I wonder what it is that I regret, what I could want to live for? I've traveled, but not everywhere I wanted. I wanted to go to Africa, to Bali, to know France and speak French for real, to speak Italian. To live in Greece. To be a hit in Paris. To write. I don't know what. To win an Academy Award. To build a home. To work in wood. To have a theatre company and do good work. To write a symphony. To make a lot of money. To live in Kyoto. To make a wonderful movie, like Miss 1000 Spring Blossoms. To build wonderful low-cost apartment buildings that work to create beauty, nature, friendship and community. To market great healthy food. To help Mom to have that restaurant. To do anything to make them both happy. Build them a house. To really deal with issues and important thoughts of life today in works of art. To add to the world's faith by disseminating my credo. To beat AIDS. To be a beacon for others to help them believe it can be done and that the spiritual is real. To write my life—in real honesty, all the sexual warts and all. I wish I had been more courageous, less a nervous wreck. A better actor. Less critical of myself, less depressive, unstable. But just as searching. I don't have many "achievements" but many satisfactions. I don't think life is about achievements

76

anyway. Look at Richard. We will all treasure him but objectively he was a minor player. It scares me to say that I am satisfied with my life but upon review, I am.

November 26—on plane home from West Coast tour of San Francisco, Seattle and Eugene

The Future:...Let me start by writing--I like this style I'm playing with where I don't censor and let my thoughts play, contradictions, irony, naivete, wisdom, cliche, originality, a melange of all that is really going on in my head. Unapologetic. Writing--it would be lovely if I just released it...letting my voice and my thoughts out to affect the world. The story of my group, of my life, of my Father's life. Even some fun porno or romance. A wonderful film idea, a gift for dialogue. Developing TV ideas, documentaries, programs for Canadian TV, what about songs? I get that heaviness, hard work feeling but I can break that.

It's a wonderful outlet for my momentary perception— flying into Eugene yesterday in the rain I saw a small community set in the rolling richly colored, chequered fields. Off in the distance the sky was clearing and creating Cecil B DeMille visual lighting effects with clouds. I thought the sun would feel cold and damp down there but the smells of the earth would be rich. I wanted very much to slip the agenda of my life and go there, see who they all were and what their lives were about. That town felt so real and tangible, so important for that moment. People think we see the world but really we just city hop, crossing thousands of miles of land and lives to another asphalt landing pad. Our society is urban obsessed and I am caught up in that obsession both willingly and unwillingly.

What else? The future—"man, what a concept" (said like Bart Simpson.) I'd love to direct. To prove my mettle. To make some really good thing appear on stage. To throw away the ideas of success, fear, etc and do shows for the good in them both for casts and crew and for audience. To be rigorous in ideals. This would be a great challenge and fun. And I'm needed—I have a classical background and could give a lot to young performers and old alike.

Maybe music would be projects then. Special things, soundtracks, themesongs, weekend things, maybe not—maybe I'll learn the piano and start to compose instrumental music. It's the words that sometimes trip me up, my melodic invention outstrips the poet in me. I'd love to have something to do with dance, making something wonderful. An acappella score? I'd like to gather some of my song ideas and pitch them to the group—Flesh, Kyoto, and the two new ones. I want us to have more weight.

I want to cut away anything that isn't in contact with the heart of life. I want to do things for the right reasons. This is my true feeling but I can't resist the image of these words being found beside the body, gun still smoking in his hand. It would be fun to finally move on the marketing of the Cosmic burger and start the ZAP! concession. Just creating it would be fun. All the healthy drinks and foods made to resemble fast food. I'd love to work with Ian to create a country home, something we've dreamed of for years. We'd need money. That's also possible. What if I gave myself permission to have significant amounts of money. It scares me a little but wouldn't it be lovely?

...I want to spend some real time on Kauai. I would love to have some land there, celebrate the art and music. I'm drawn to art of the South West as well.

To espouse my spiritual beliefs—to witness. To create some art that deals directly. Suddenly thought of a two-tiered story in present and in medieval times during plague—Narcissus and Goldmund—times. Two plagues.

Some fount of knowledge that reassures, some oracular personage...

Maybe write a film...

Learn to paint. Or just paint.

February 7, 1991—Boise, Idaho

Healing. Reading Beyond Aids. Like a magic book into my hands the day after Barry and I have a talk about my refusal to love myself and my disconnection from the source of all Energy. This book says it for me. But have I got the guts to look my fears in the face? Do I believe in my true Identity—do I yearn to know it? I do know that life as an ego-directed self is turning into a dead end.

My first exercise: beliefs.

Tonight: my body, my illness.

Medical science tells me:

-there is no cure

-it is invariably fatal

-it is powerful

-no cure in sight, little known, tricky virus

-2 to 10 yrs

-alternative healing is balderdash for gullible, desperate people

-it is caused by a virus

Other beliefs about this illness—

-it is a punishment

-it is unclean

-it is sexual, a shameful retribution for sexual practices

-it attacks people who are at a dead end in their lives

-it ATTACKS, I am a victim

-I am guilty of not caring for myself—I don't eat right, don't exercise, and harbor depressed thoughts about my chances

-I work too hard for my good health

-I think all that stuff about stress and mind is bullshit. I'm gonna die from it and that's that.

My body—is eaten up by it

-is weak

-is unable to fight back

-has betrayed me

-is a sad thing

-has become so ugly

-is falling apart

-has some recuperative powers, is intelligent and resilient when cooperated with

-has lost its good looks forever

-is old

-needs the AZT

-nothing will help it, it's hopeless

-I deserve it. I brought it on myself with my guilt, the hatred and fear etc I felt for Paul C.

-there is lots of love and sympathy for me from many people—I must have been a nice guy

-I must be brave and noble, keep going with a smile, protecting everyone from the deep pain and hopelessness I feel

-my good health, looks, energy are all past

-I'm killing myself by my neglect, self-abuse and hopelessness

-the group is using me

Affirmations to change my beliefs—

-I can cure myself of this illness

-the causes are deeper than the virus and are at my control

-I am the UNLIMITED, HOLY SON of GOD and I can create any reality I wish

-I am powerful, the disease is weak and easily affected

-By referring all healing methods to my intuition I will know what works for me.

-This disease is a message to change my beliefs, my heart, my way of life

-I am not a victim, I am the creator

-This disease is a loving message from the Universe that I must change. It is loving not a punishment.

-I am the sinless, holy son of God. There can be no cause for punishment, guilt is an illusion on my part.

-It may appear when [that?] a person is stuck but it is a loving message to change and to grow into a new wonderful life based on love and my TRUE IDENTITY

-Sex is good. SEX is GOOD. SEX is GOD. I must release the sense of guilt over my sexual feelings, orientation and experiences—that is what's harmful.

-Nothing gives me greater joy than to care for myself. My every thought is a healing thought.

-I am certain of success

-I live a balanced life with time for all my needs and healing

-My thoughts have a direct effect on my body and my health. I can create perfect health, a healthy strong attractive body.

-My body is as strong or weak as I create it. It has all the recuperative powers I need.

-My body needs no potions or pills, no magic charms but it does need a heart completely filled with love and forgiveness.

-I am innocent, guiltless, sinless. It is impossible that I can be guilty of anything.

   -I am emotionally honest with myself, realizing this is the door to true healing. I am willing to look my fears in the eye and change them with love.

-I am activating the greatest Power in the Universe. I cannot fail.

-The best days of my life are yet to come.

-I am healing myself by my self-love, caring and faith.

-I am the beloved Son of God; perfect health and abundance are mine.

Thursday Feb 28 [at a healing spa in Rimrock, AZ]

I love myself.

Got some good sleep last night altho the coffee buzzes me for about an hour. Still with three periods 8-11, 12-3, 4-7 there's something approximating a night's sleep. Graham the Kiwi cook is a lovely man and we enjoy talking. His wife does makeup for Madonna. He has those beautiful Maori features.

I wish to deal with all the guilt and shame and despair of the years with Paul and the breakup. Let me look at that dark black ball and see if its components will reveal themselves:

I see myself as guilty of

Cowardice/not standing up to him—not venting my rage but talking behind the scenes.

Anger—outrage, self-righteousness

Jealousy—of his easiness, playfulness, his leadership qualities

Plotting—to win, to foil his plot

Revenge—hungering for it, gleeful when anything went our way and he lost when his songs weren't picked

hard-heartedness—no sympathy for what he must have been going through

attacking—seeing attack and returning same mocking him behind his back

superiority—assuming the supreriority of our ideas, heaping scorn on anything "they" said

competitiveness—always between

us—one of us trying to put the other down to win, to show him

depression—losing interest in life

82

fearfulness—so much fear held inside eating at me, fear of
the group breaking, of me out on my own, of the album
or whatever not being "good enough"
judgemental—he's fat, he bellows, his taste is low class and
common, he embarrasses me, he's evil

Inner Dialogue Work Fri 8th

I'm not a truly original composer like the guy who wrote
the song I'm listening to on the radio with its leaps of
originality—I'm structured, safe and not that talented.

I'm a broken down bag of bones.

But my rib's better some.

My lungs are bad—they make that sound.

Do I believe that I am unlimited and God's Son?

Are crystals a load of crap? I felt something today.

This body paint is working

Yes I believe my Father hears me

It's about degradation, guilt, punishment, tragedy,
wanting to heal but not knowing how to do it inside.

I know there's an outside chance I can heal myself. Is it
me who heals?

My ass is bony and hurts to sit long.

Emotional release tape was so good—unburdened.

George Melton coming—will he help me? Do it for
me?

No but I see him as above me—he's done it.

I want to hide my lesions so people don't freak out. Or
so I can pretend it's not there, denial as I did for so long this
last year.

The lesions are God's judgement on me, that I am bad. Embarrassment because

I can't control them, I'm falling apart, coming unglued

They seem so strong, so heedless of what I want.

It's a horror story that they're on my face.

I see the start of another cluster on my left shin and suddenly I am seized with a terror. I have no control, I'm helpless, it will do as it wishes, eventually ending up like the other. I am trapped in a horror show.

It's so easy to be a patsy for all this positive thinking. I see myself through my father's eyes babbling on about God healing me and seeing how sad I look with the reality being I'm getting sicker.

My body: I've been able to ask great feats of stamina. It is strong and keeps going. My chest is weak—my doing self—and my arms—the masculine take charge control self—but my legs and back are strong, stamina.

When I get sick I suddenly see myself as weak and helpless.

I'm tired all the time. What worries me? That I'll sink deeper and deeper and never come out.

Western medicine can be a good thing.

Ian Wallace

Marc's longtime companion; this is the text of a speech he gave in Vancouver on AIDS and loss

Hello everybody, my name is Ian Wallace. My partner for 17 years was Marc Connors. Some of you may have heard Marc sing with The Nylons at Malkin Bowl here in Vancouver which he loved so much. He told me about an amazing acid trip he experienced right here in this gazebo in 1968, so I feel very honored and privileged to be sharing this story here tonight.

We were both diagnosed HIV positive in 1986, as well I had Kaposi Sarcoma [KS] which meant I had AIDS, and was told by the doctor that I might have six months to live. In those days nobody really knew much at all so we proceeded to educate ourselves. We came to embrace the challenge of AIDS in our lives as an opportunity to live according to our belief in the healing power of the mind. We undertook an intensive program of cleansing, fasting, meditation, juicing, Chinese herbs, acupuncture, QI kung, Vitamin C IV, Ozone therapy, etc. etc. Marc carried his juicer with him on tour and boiled up foul-smelling concoctions of Chinese roots, bark, beetles and berries in his hotel rooms. We had decided against taking AZT or any other Pharmaceuticals and that we would never have chemotherapy or radiation.

Four years went by. My KS slowly progressed and I still expected that I might die in the next six months—Marc looked gorgeous, radiant and healthy, performing and recording, touring Japan, Australia, Europe and all over Canada and the U.S. I was glad that it was me who was going to die first because I didn't think I could face the death of my beautiful man and be left to contend on my own. However, one day he asked me to look at some red spots that had appeared on his body. They turned out to be KS and proceeded to flare up very quickly. Where mine had been very slow in developing, his was like wildfire. It started to appear on his face, causing swelling and distortion. Marc continued to appear in public, performing and recording, but hiding behind a mask of makeup that took him at least an hour to apply before he would go out of the house. It was heartbreaking for me to watch him. His face became so ravaged and distorted that people didn't recognize him. Immediately after recording his final album we went to a healing spa in Arizona for an intensive cleansing program which was like a last resort for him. I started to feel better, but Marc continued to get worse. When we got back to Toronto he was very weak and on oxygen. His parents and sister drove down from Kingston and sat with him. After they left he said it was the most difficult thing he had ever done—sitting there seeing the look of terror on the faces of his family.

From the time they left, until the ambulance arrived the next morning to take us to the clinic, he went into a kind of trance state where he was chanting in an undefinable language, I heard him talking to some entity as if he was receiving instructions. I felt like I was in a bizarre dream. The journey in the ambulance through downtown Toronto, into the elevator with gawking crowds, I was so relieved when we arrived at the clinic on the 26th floor—the nurses loved him so much and he felt totally safe there. As they were lifting him off the gurney onto the bed I was telling Paula, our favorite nurse, how he had been over the weekend. Next moment I hear a flurry of activity, they're pounding on his chest, giving mouth to mouth—I just gasped—he's gone. He had hung on until we got to the clinic where he felt safe enough to surrender. I was in shock. This was my biggest fear.

As I looked at his body the most amazing thing happened—I felt myself being gently enveloped in the most beautiful, loving, protective energy. It totally surrounded me and permeated every cell of my body and consciousness. I recognized the feeling immediately—it was Marc—his presence, his radiant smile, his love was right inside my heart and all around me. I touched his body, it was still warm, but Marc wasn't there any more—he was infused in me, he was holding me, comforting me. I wasn't afraid any more, I had no sense of loss.

His light, his presence within me allowed me to conduct the most amazing celebratory funeral service—people were uplifted, there was tremendous joy and laughter. I was taken into such a high plane of consciousness—there was nothing for me to grieve—my friend was present in my heart. Some people were angry with me for not being upset. How could I be upset, I had just faced the most fearful thing I ever thought I could, and in the process received a gift of divine proportion—the tangible experience of the living spirit of my beloved Marc.

I ask us all to see beyond the body—to see each other as we truly are—immortal, infinite, abundant beings of light. We are all one. Thank you.

Made in the USA
Monee, IL
06 April 2024